PRAISE FOR FAY JACOBS' BOOKS

For Frying Out Loud —

National Federation of Press Women Non-Fiction Book of the Year
Winner! ForeWord Reviews Book of the Year — Honorable
   Mention Humor
Winner! Delaware Press Association Humor Book of the Year
Winner! Golden Crown Literary Society — Essays/Short Stories
Nominee! American Library Association Over the Rainbow
   Award
Finalist! Independent Publishers IPPY Award for Non-Fiction
Finalist: Ann Bannon Readers' Choice Award

"Her columns...are laugh out loud funny and the best part is
that Jacobs is sincere...those who enjoyed Jacobs' first collection will not be disappointed and those reading her for the first
time will understand why she's such a beloved
columnist." — **Jane van Ingen, Lambda Book Report**

"It's an intelligent, hysterically funny and occasionally poignant
look at how we live today, with hopes for tomorrow.
Recommended for everyone, male or female, gay or straight.
Five stars out of five." — **Echo Magazine**

"Fay's essays resonate with warmth, candid humor, and the
unabashed joy of finding one's place." — **OUTtraveler.**

"Every bit as sardonic, witty, sarcastic and insightful as her first
book." — **Richard LaBonte, San Francisco Bay Times**

"Fay Jacob's hilarious dispatches are funny, touching—and
real. This is a true laugh riot, as Fay wittily takes on sexuality,
politics, relationships, and day-to-day dilemmas." — **Insight
Out Book Club**

Every tale is masterfully told—these memorable memoirs...
are both pleasure and treasure." — **Anna Furtado,
JustAboutWrite**

"Fay Jacobs' books are part memoir, part social commentary, and an easy and fun summer read. Very smart, very funny, very insightful. These books will appeal to everyone. — **Northampton's Pride and Joy Bookstore**

"She has the sarcastic wit of the best political commentators, and little that has occurred in the past few years escapes her piercing pen...Get your copy of her books. Perfect summer (or anytime) reading. — **Chelsea Pines Inn Newsletter**

Time Fries!

AGING GRACELESSLY IN REHOBOTH BEACH

Time Fries!

AGING GRACELESSLY IN REHOBOTH BEACH

By Fay Jacobs

A&M Books

2013

A&M BOOKS

Time Fries!
Aging Gracelessly in Rehoboth Beach
By Fay Jacobs

Printed in the United States of America
First Edition

Cover and book design by Murray Archibald
Typeset by Steve Elkins

ISBN 978-0-983-7961-5-2

Also by the author
As I Lay Frying – a Rehoboth Beach Memoir
Fried & True – Tales from Rehoboth Beach
For Frying Out Loud – Rehoboth Beach Diaries

To BJQ and the Usual Suspects, along with the two party boys who made much of this possible.

Foreword

BY ERIC C. PETERSON

Good mothers tell you everything you need to know so you'll lead a full and happy life. The very best mothers, on the other hand, simply lead full and happy lives themselves, and trust that their kids have enough sense to watch and learn.

I have three such mothers. When I tell you that one of them is Catholic and two of them are Jewish, you'll appreciate that I've had my share of advice in my life. And while much of the advice has been wonderful, I've learned the most from simply watching them live.

And here are some of the most important things I've learned by observation:

1) Friends are the most important thing. And kindness is the most important trait.

2) Say what's on your mind. Most of your friends will agree with you and the ones who don't will forgive you if you really matter to them, and if they can't, they shouldn't let the door hit 'em in the ass as they exit your life.

3) When you're young, Mimosas and Bloody Mary's are socially acceptable cocktails to drink in the morning because they contain various kinds of juice. However, you will reach a certain age wherein the acid reflux caused by the Mimosa's orange juice and the high-blood pressure resulting from the oversalted Bloody Mary tomato juice outweighs the evils of drink, and it's easier just to order champagne or a vodka stinger and be done with it.

4) Skunks are never too young to spray. Never.

What you're about to read is the story of one of my mothers — with frequent guest appearances by a second, her loving spouse. It's actually a lot of stories, but there's a common thread about getting older. It's about all the little ways her body is beginning to betray her, all the times she forgets that she's not 30 anymore, forgets how to act her age, and forgets where the hell she put her car keys. It's the story of a woman approaching her golden years with style, verve, and not a shred of dignity.

And it makes me so proud.

No, honest. I should be having this much fun when my eyebrows have grown to resemble North American Grizzly Caterpillars and my prostate blows up like a balloon. Hell, I should be having this much fun right this minute; we all should. But very few of us do. We should all have a modern-day Auntie Mame to show us the way, but very few of us do. But I do.

And if I do say so myself, it's awfully big of me to share her with you.

Eric C. Peterson

Table of Contents

2013

Introduction

As much as they say the sixties are the new forties, I'm not so sure.

Jamie Lee Curtis is constipated, Tommy Lee Jones has a reverse mortgage so he can stay home until he dies, and Quarterback Joe Theismann has no testosterone. Have you seen these commercials? How did this happen?

I just saw a t-shirt with a graphic in the shape of that little plastic gizmo we used to play 45 rpm records. The shirt said, "If you recognize this, you're a geezer." Guilty. By association. Say, wasn't it The Association…or maybe the Beach Boys…singing, "God Only Knows Where I'd Be Without You?" In the 60s it was about true love. Now it's God Only Knows where I'd be without you reminding me twelve times I've got a dentist appointment.

Most days I feel young, adventurous and bold, until I'm at the threshold of a room, wondering what I've come to retrieve. Last week I calmly put breakfast in the microwave, had coffee, left home, and returned hours later to a cold rubbery omelet I could use for a doggie chew toy. And at five bucks a gallon I'm crazed by the amount of gas I use just riding back to the house to see if I closed the garage door.

After years of boating in the sunshine I have a cataract. It can be removed, right? No. Some insurance company bozo tells me it isn't ripe yet. What am I a tomato? While I'm ripening, my eyesight is so bad I cannot see the chin hairs I'm sprouting.

Okay, and whatever you do, promise me you will never, ever put a magnifying mirror down on a flat surface, bend over and gaze into it. My God, gravity exacts its toll and I look like a Char Pei.

Have you been to an organ recital? You know, evenings where all your friends start reciting which of their bodily organs are deteriorating. Who thought I'd ever spend more time talking about meniscus than money, polyps than politics, reflux than religion. We used to speculate about who was naughty, and might be into S&M and handcuffs. Now it's all about colon health and rotator cuffs.

Do you sinus wash? It's all the rage for avoiding germs and staying healthy. You take a little plastic pitcher with a watering can spout and siphon saline solution and warm water up your nose. Try it and you'll understand the horror of water boarding. I think I got the Dick Cheney model.

Which brings me to heart health. So far so good. But last week we were at a party where somebody at our table had a tiny oxygen meter he'd clip to his finger to test his oxygen level. Naturally, we all had to pass it around and see if we were still alive. E.T. Call Home. My god, I remember the days when we'd all pass around a nickel bag of weed; now we're passing an oxygen meter. Please don't tell Mick Jagger.

Or, for that matter, don't tell Gloria Vanderbilt how many times in the last six months I have gotten dressed in the morning only to discover, once out in natural light, I'm wearing black pants and a navy shirt. And don't get me started about clothing. Trying to find attractive age-appropriate garments is like trying to find a drag queen at NASCAR. All the fashionistas think they're doing a good thing by making trendy looking clothes in large sizes. Those huggy, midriff showing lacy things look great on Snooki and the Kardashians but trust me, nobody wants to see a baby boomer belly button.

And those commercials! For every advertised remedy, the side effects are a gazillion times the benefits. Am I alone here, not wanting to swallow something that warns "infections, some fatal, may occur?"

Which all goes to say that I'm feeling my age. Or am I? I'm so far past menopause I'm symptom free with not so much as a hot-flashback. I've stuck with the gym, continue to play lousy golf and feel pretty darn healthy. My friends are having civil unions left and right, many simultaneously celebrating 25 and

30 year anniversaries. We're all up on the dance floor, hands waving in the air, dancing to "I Will Survive" and "I Like the Night Life."

What the dickens, it's the youngest times, it's the oldest times. I like it.▼

September 2010

My mate and I upend our lives every decade or so. For new readers, I'll catch you up: In the 80s we bought a boat (a hole in the water into which you throw money); in the 90s we moved said vessel to Rehoboth Bay (Dewey Beach drunks and steel drums at 1 a.m. UGH!); at Millennium's dawn we moved ourselves full-time to Rehoboth (okay, so who needs a decent paying job anyway?); and now we are on the move and downwardly mobile once again. Ever financially imprudent, we now own a great big depreciating asset—a 27-foot recreational vehicle.

And while the land yacht lifestyle is fantastic, it has a learning curve. We're still in first grade.

Frankly, it's a good thing we took to RVing instantly, because on Day One, we had only 45 minutes of flight instruction before leaving Tampa, FL for the journey home in the Hindenburg. Amateurs, rev your engines.

My spouse drove fearlessly; me riding shotgun. We were lucky not to take out mailboxes and parked cars on both sides of the street as our blimp lumbered towards I-95. But within minutes, my mate had expertly judged the big rig's midsection, checked out the giant funhouse mirrors flanking the bus and learned to love the back-up camera. We set out at 8 a.m. and by noon we were maneuvering it like a Mini-Cooper, tooling down the road with the Schnauzers asleep in their beds on the floor.

Lesson One: Like a boat, it is prudent to secure all contents when underway. Braking for a red light sent a 2-lb bag of M&M Peanuts bouncing, then rolling into every crevice in the vehicle, immediately followed by occupied doggie beds sliding and twisting forward like Olympic curling stones. From now on, we batten the hatches and seat belt the dogs.

Lesson Two: At our first campground they assigned us site

57, Kilimanjaro. With the left side of the camper listing to port, we broke out the wood chocks (*how much wood could a wood chock chock if a…*), put them under the left side tires and backed up onto them. After several daring tries ("back up, no, go forward, *STOP*, you're not back far enough, oh, hell, now you've driven over the chock…") we were still caddywhompus but parked. When we went inside for martinis, it was a little like cocktails on the Titanic.

Lesson Three: Upon our return we stopped at a local campground for a sewer hook-up. I was enlisted to stand with my foot holding down the hose while we emptied our tank. Once I was firmly in place my co-pilot ran, laughing, 50 yards away from the stench. Next time I will hold my breath as I hold my mate over the hole.

Lesson Four (*corollary to Lesson One*)**:** These RV newbies didn't have any idea how to stow our stuff. I bought closet organizers with little cubby holes for shoes, shirts and shorts. Every time we stopped the rig, gravity lurched the clothes forward and every night, we opened the cabinets to an avalanche. Our digs looked like a reality TV hoarder episode. Trolling Walmart for a solution, I bought a pair of old geezer suspenders, stretched them from top to bottom in the closet and kept our shorts and shirts tucked in. It's a look.

Lesson Five: Before you unhook the car you've been towing behind the RV, engage the car's emergency brake. Kneecapping yourself is no way to start happy hour.

Lesson Six: Make a pact: no yelling. Then buy walkie talkies so nobody else hears the inevitable yelling. And plan 45 minutes for disembarkation—detaching, disengaging and otherwise undoing yourself from plugs, hoses and bung holes. With most couples there's the doer and one who watches the doer do. I just stand around holding the bag with the pins and chocks and pliers, etc. That's me, left holding the bag.

Lesson Seven: Campsites, regardless of their marketing brochures go from the sublime to the ridiculous. One day we're nestled in a tree-canopied site overlooking a gorgeous rocky ocean cove, then we're sleeping in a gravel-filled parking lot overlooking somebody's rusty double-wide. We've relaxed at quiet sites down by the old mill stream (literally) or atop mountains with wild turkeys running around. Then we wind up back to back, belly to belly with a hundred rigs in parks resembling Saturday morning on Route One. When somebody sneezes, you hear a dozen "Bless Yous." Or, there are worse things you overhear, just sayin'.

Lesson Eight: GPS is not perfect, MapQuest often has its pants on fire. Once, as we searched for a campground we were pointed to a sign boasting camping/landfill. Houston, we have a problem! A night atop Mt. Trashmore is not my idea of luxury accommodations.

Lesson Nine: Boondoggling (staying someplace free, without electric, water or sewer) has its challenges. Walmart is a famous boondoggling site, as are some highway rest stops. But when we slept at the 24-hour Walmart, I couldn't sleep. People were shopping. I kept hearing car doors slam. I knew people were carrying purchases. No rest for the weary shopaholic. It was like being in detox. So much for boondoggling.

Lesson Ten: That which doesn't kill us makes us RVers.

From Chincoteague to Amish country, Maine to as far as Nova Scotia, we've had grand adventures so far. Besides, the bus can be an annex for overflow summer guests. And we never know when it might be prudent to get out of Dodge ahead of a hurricane or tourist flash mob.

With our load levelers, e-z hitches, clamps, coils, hoses, walkie talkies and thirsty gas tank (a hole in the highway into which you pour money?) we should probably have our heads examined. But here we are, planning the next excursion.

Closets wearing suspenders? Check!

Schnauzers seat-belted in? Check!

Wide loads secured in the wide load? Check!

Rollin', Rollin', Rollin', keep those doggies rollin'... ▼

October 2010

I do not feel old. But apparently I am.

The other day I went to buy tickets for the RB Film Fest. It's one of my favorite days of the year, standing in line with the regulars outside the Film Society office on the first day of sales. I get to see people I haven't seen in 365 days, picking up conversations like it was yesterday. This year, the society staff handed out numbers to us early birds and put out a bunch of chairs.

So there I am, walking up to the throng, and a woman seated in one of the chairs looks in my direction and asks, "Do you need a seat?"

I looked behind me to see who she was talking to. I was alone.

Okay, the woman may have been a few years, or perhaps decades younger than me, but did I really look like I couldn't loiter upright for a half hour? Hell, I once stood in line for eleven hours for Billy Joel tickets. The operative word is probably "once," as in "upon a time." Crap.

Later, the UPS truck pulled up with a package from Bonnie's doctor. It was an inflatable device to be used in the bedroom. Now before you start gagging and hollering TMI, listen to this: it's a blow-up wedgie for the head of the bed to help with digestion. That's right, an anti-Reflux device.

To be clear, I only have reflux in two situations—first, drinking a Mimosa. It's not the bubbly, it's the acidic juice. So now I just have straight champagne, no problem. The only other time I get reflux is when I see Karl Rove on TV, and who doesn't?

However, my mate does suffer from the occasional bad night caused by food and beverage. Hence, instead of putting unsightly phone books under the legs at the head of the bed, we've installed an unsightly inflatable airplane chute.

I'd like to say that the last time I inflated something at bedtime it was a blow-up doll, but I was never that naughty. Now, we pump up the wedgie to raise the head of the mattress and try, just try to get into bed. With half the length of the bed propped up by a beach ball, you have to be a gymnast to get into the sack. The first time we tried, it was like high jumping onto a waterbed. Then we had to figure out how to sleep sitting up and laughing.

But that was easy compared to what happened when I got out of bed to turn off the hall light. Bonnie, remaining somewhat prone, saw her side of the wedgie mattress suddenly deflate, while my side shot up like Space Mountain. I'd have to pole vault to get back in. I suggested that my spouse roll to the middle to give me a fighting chance. A rope and mountain climbing crampons might have helped, but I finally hoisted myself back aboard.

Unfortunately, the incident repeated itself when Bonnie got up to pee at 3 a.m. With no warning at all, my side of the bed went limp and a Schnauzer rolled off, followed closely by most of me. It would have been all of me but I grabbed the headboard and hauled myself back up Pike's Peak. Doing chin-ups on the headboard is not my idea of bedtime relaxation. Okay, so there will be no more "now I lay me down to sleep at our house." It's like spending the night on K2.

My being a mountain goat aside, I refuse to believe I'm actually as old as it says on my driver's license. I mean Bonnie complains that I still have more energy than the Washington Redskins. Although I don't think she's referring to how well they run the ball, but how well I run my mouth.

Even so, there are insidious reminders of my biological age cropping up everywhere. Today in Walmart I didn't recognize any of the singers on the CDs labeled just released, but I found Simon and Garfunkel dumped in the bargain bin. Then I saw that most of the stuff in my shopping cart said "for speedy relief." Would I remember where my car was in the parking lot? Would

|I drive home with my left turn signal blinking the entire way? Could this really be happening to me?

Well, the answer is yes. And no. While it's sad but true that in an antique store the other day I heard myself say "I remember these," I maintain that I am not your typical aging boomer.

I dressed up for Halloween, I do not eat dinner at 4 p.m. (okay, there is the sushi happy hour where you have to order by 6 p.m.), and nobody has to worry about calling my house at 9 p.m. and asking "did I wake you?"

Also on the plus side, the criminal amount I've paid in health insurance is my only investment that's starting to pay off. The other day a comic said old people have it pretty good–in a hostage situation we're most likely to be released first. That's comforting.

But the real trick is having the best of both worlds. I may be retired from 9-5, but I'm working harder than ever as a full-time writer and publisher—and loving it. It also doesn't hurt going to the mailbox once a month and getting a government check.

But the trick to navigating this getting older thing is knowing exactly when to cave. Recently, a great big truck backed into my driveway (shameless plug alert!) and delivered thousands of copies of my book, *For Frying Out Loud— Rehoboth Beach Diaries*. In preparation, using age and experience to advantage, I contracted with several strapping young women to move cartons around while I stood and watched. I even sat in a beach chair to ogle. Although, I repeat, nobody needs to get up to give me a seat on the subway or anywhere else. Ask, and I'll slap you.

I'm off to grab a Sherpa guide Schnauzer and scale Mount Kilimanjaro on the way to bed. "Hey, Bon, roll to the middle." ▼

THE BOOK FAIR THAT GOT MY GOAT

With my book publishing business I can go from sublime to ridiculous in a flash.

Since my three books all started as columns, I feel like I'm talking to family when I report how things are going. And they are going great. The reception I've gotten here at home for the new book has been wonderful. Books are flying out of my garage warehouse from sales, both online and in line at local bookstore signings. I'm humbled and happy.

But possibly to ensure that my head doesn't bloat I have been treated to some matchless experiences hawking the books—and a book tour, however delightful New York, Chicago, or P-Town can be, has its ups and downs.

Literally. I've traipsed up and down creaky staircases lugging cartons of books until I've actually screamed "for frying out loud!" And I've survived readings for just a handful of hardy audience members, filled out, fortunately by my own blood relatives.

And all the travel isn't exactly glamorous. Thank goodness for GPS when I found myself careening through the narrow streets of Staten Island, NY, seeking a tiny LGBT bookstore sandwiched between Household of Love Church and Our Lady of Pity Ministries. Loved the owners, loved the crowd, can't say much for the neighborhood.

Not that I'm having an Our Lady of Pity party. It's been a real blast networking at book conferences and meeting readers in bookstores, signing and selling lots of books. Gay Days at Disney was a hoot, and at some readings I get laughs like I was doing stand-up. Of course, Women's Week in P-Town was grand.

Then again, it's sobering to be partying with readers and selling books Saturday night to find myself reading on Sunday in a dark, dank, mostly empty bar, still reeking of the previous night's beer blast. Oh, that would be the bar reeking of beer, not me. Then again, it was Women's Week P-Town, so who's to judge?

But it wasn't hard to be judgmental about a book fair in Dover at the Delaware Agricultural Museum, a place, as you can imagine, I had no idea even existed. It houses antique tractors, cotton gins, and all manner of rural artifacts. And it sits across the street from the NASCAR track, which might have been a clue for urban me.

I arrived to discover I was to set up my display in front of the museum's goat breed exhibit, which I found instantly hilarious and appropriate. After dragging a six-foot folding table, a lawn chair, and several book cartons from the parking lot to the door, I felt pretty much like an old goat myself.

As I unpacked, I noticed I was underdressed. There were authors in full Civil War garb, writers who appeared to be dressed for a White House state dinner, and a couple of women who might have been palm readers and/or still dressed for Trick or Treat.

The man next to me boasted of having published 30 different volumes about Hessian soldiers in the Revolutionary War, though his plastic spiral-bound books seemed to have been published by Kinko House.

I was surrounded by authors peddling badly bound copies of books with titles like *Last Chance for Jesus* and *Sex with Unicorns—How I Talk to God*.

A young woman came up to my table, read a blurb about A&M Books and asked, "What exactly is a feminist press?" I sized her up. She seemed to have most of her teeth and wasn't dressed for a Rebel encampment so I took a chance.

"Actually, it's a lesbian press, but in the 70s no printer would touch a lesbian book," I answered. The woman said nothing but actually took a giant step back, apparently afraid to catch, as Rachel Maddow says, "the gay."

Once everybody was set up, a dribble of patrons came through the doors. People would walk by, pick up my book, smile at the cover and turn it over to read the back. I could tell the exact moment they got to the word gay. They plopped the book down like it had cooties.

Instead of twiddling my thumbs waiting for somebody to come up and insult me I spent time checking out the goat display. Goats are kept for milk, meat, or hair, and some are also kept as companions. All goat breeds are very hardy, curious, and intelligent. Hey, maybe they'd like to read some essays or at least eat the book cover. Nothing else was happening.

One woman flipped through my book, stopped, looked up and said "You wrote 'pray for Obama Care', I really can't talk to you, you're a Commie." She slammed the book down as if it contained Anthrax. It made me want to back up and get in the pen with the intelligent taxidermied goats.

One bright spot had a man picking up the book, oohing and ahhing at the photo and then saying "Wow, that's a beautiful dog. Cocker Spaniel?" If he couldn't tell the difference between a Cocker and a Schnauzer, what hope was there for his understanding a lesbian smartass?

I was buoyed by a man making a beeline for my table but it turned out he wanted to read about Nubian Dairy Goats. Then I got nervous when the Civil War author unsheathed his sword brandishing it about for people to admire. I'd only been there two hours, and had a stupefying two more to go. I considered grabbing the sword and falling on it.

Finally, a lady came by, picked up the book, turned it over and read the entire back of the book and said, *"For Frying Out Loud.* Um…Is it a cookbook? What do you fry?"

Exit cue.

I came back to Rehoboth to discover that while I was sitting on my butt trying to peddle books to homophobes and religious zealots, I'd sold 20 books here at home at Proud Bookstore. It's so nice to have a niche to come home to.

Next, I'm off to Giovanni's Room, a LGBT bookstore in Philly. I expect my experience there will be a welcoming one. While we can't always count on patrons or book buyers to be in good moods, if anybody is grumpy or gruff, at least I'm fairly certain nobody will be Billy Goat Gruff.

At least I hope not.▼

April 2011

It's a hoax. This whole business of wireless communication is one big fat lie. While the communication may be wireless, its facilitation requires enough wires, cables and plugs to gag a landfill.

And of course, chargers last eons longer than the devices they power. I have souvenir chargers from every cell phone, iPod and laptop I've ever owned, plus miles of random cords from USB data cables, external hard drives, headphones and digital cameras. And heaven forbid a new device should use a leftover charger from an old device. Someday they'll find me hog tied and buried in wireless wires. It's just oxymoronic with the emphasis on moronic.

I say this, crouched on the floor, wedged under my desk, trying to plug in my dying cell phone so I won't lose my turn in the endless "on hold" cue for Verizon.

I'm calling to ask why my Droid has the battery life of a piss ant, beeping and dying by lunchtime. Now I've got a Schnauzer trying to squeeze under the desk with me because he figures I'm down here sniffing for lunch crumbs.

You should have seen me one night this terrible winter in the local ER, where, fortunately, I was trying to call somebody to tell them that no, my spouse had not broken her hip, after slipping on an unsalted sidewalk.

The only plug I could use to rescue my wireless phone was in the waiting room behind a coat rack, where I had to huddle cross-legged on the floor, the hem of somebody's ski parka draped on my head. I looked like some freaky new age Buddha, but it was lucky I had my phone charger along. Well, it really wasn't luck. I keep a charger in my car, in the kitchen, in the den, and a spare stuffed in my coat pocket. Sometimes the wires hang out and I look like a suicide bomber. It's not a good fashion statement.

We packed the camper for a road trip recently and I had so many charging devices on my nightstand it looked like a pot of squid ink linguini exploded in there.

Well, at least I don't have to go to the gym. I do daily knee bends and crunches with the endless plugging and unplugging of chargers, in and out of the sockets that sadistic builders install 16 inches off the floor. For somebody my age, nothing should be just 16 inches off the floor, not even the dog.

I may not have the energy for this anymore but the electric company does. I read that power cords use electricity even when devices aren't plugged in. Apparently, only 5 percent of the power drawn by phone chargers actually charges phones, while the other 95 percent dribbles out when you leave the charger plugged in without a phone hanging on it. Who knew?

It creeps me out to feel how warm a cell phone recharger can be even when not attached to a phone. Is it dangerous? Dunno, but I worry about things like this. Now I realize that worrying doesn't solve anything but it does give me something to do until the trouble starts. And I think there could be trouble. Our next great fire won't be started by Mrs. O'Leary's Cow, but Mrs. O'Leary's iPad charger.

So now I have ten minutes added to my nightly ritual. Lock the door, put the thermostat down, let the dogs out, unplug three cell phone chargers, unplug two computers, unplug the toaster, let the dogs in, take two Ibuprofen and start over in the morning. I've turned into my grandmother.

I thought there was good news with the invention of the wireless charging pad to do away with charger wires. But no. Using the thing requires special adaptors on all your electronics, insuring, once again, that when the devices are dead you'll be left holding the bag of adaptors.

What about Bluetooth? It took me a while to get that Bluetooth referred to electronics, not dental disease, but I have since noticed that half the population walks around wearing hearing aids like Secret Service agents. It's gotten pretty hard to tell whether somebody is talking to somebody else by

Bluetooth or talking to themselves by Schizophrenia. But okay, it's all worth it because this contraption is really, really wireless.

Not so fast. Since Delaware now requires hands-free cell phone use in cars, I got a Bluetooth ear set myself. Imagine my disgust in discovering that the damn thing needs to be charged just like a cell phone. So now I've got one more stupid charger to work into my stupefying daily routine.

I did find out that my Droid car charger actually has a spare USB port in it so I can charge my phone while I drive and charge my Bluetooth device in piggy-back fashion in the same plug at the same time. I'll be lucky if I don't choke myself behind the wheel.

Pretty soon cars will come equipped with multi-outlet surge protectors for all the add-ons and accessories needed for ET to call home, and it will be built right into the car's padded arm-rest. Before then, I may well wind up in a padded cell.

Meanwhile, I'm still on hold with Verizon.

"Verizon Customer Service. May I help you?"

"Well, I hope so. I'm wondering why my Droid battery has the life expectancy of a fruit fly."

"Hmmm. What model phone…?"

At which point, as if I wasn't wired enough, I reached for my coffee cup, accidentally yanking my phone charger from the wall. Mr. Droid beeped, bleeped, then croaked. And, I became completely, irrationally, unplugged.

I'm off to call Verizon from the antique land line dumb phone. You'll find me tethered to the kitchen. What wireless??? If smart phones are so smart, let them solve this problem. Just don't hold your breath.▼

May 2011

It's been a month of highs and highers for me since my last column, with just one or two dips from the euphoria.

First, for me, the Rehoboth Beach Women's FEST was a blast, just as I hope it was for the many hundreds of women who attended. Comic Jennie McNulty really enjoyed her introduction to Rehoboth and can't wait to come back. We took her out on the town after her performance and all our watering holes were packed. We did get to crash a bachelorette party at one of our cherished spots, watching drunken straight gals pole dance, show their thongs, and otherwise behave in an embarrassing way.

"We've come a long way," said Jennie. "The gay people are in a corner laughing at the straight people."

Far be it from me to indict a whole class of people for the behavior of a few, but just like we have our assholes, they have theirs—and a gaggle of theirs were on display.

What I will take away from the weekend (besides the awesome crowds, money raised with the Broadwalk for Breast Cancer on the Boardwalk, and so much more) is a strategy Jennie suggested we use from now on. In her show she told us just how to get gay marriage passed in this country. "Lie," she said, "just like the opposition does with their made up statistics about the horrors gay people cause." She said, "Just say that erectile dysfunction in men goes down dramatically with the rise of gay marriage." Ha! More brilliant advice I could not invent.

And speaking of marriage, in Delaware, starting January 1, 2012, gay couples will have all the civil rights afforded to married couples. In a brilliantly orchestrated campaign by Equality Delaware, and our wonderful House Majority Leader Pete Schwartzkopf, civil unions passed the Delaware General Assembly almost before the homophobes and hate-mongers had a chance to rev their despicable engines.

17

While it took eight long years to pass the anti-discrimination bill, thanks to great legal preparation and a massive team lobbying on the ground, Civil Union legislation passed in a mere few months.

If you didn't have the pleasure of being at Legislative Hall on that Thursday evening in April to hear the debate and watch the final vote, let me give you an image of what it was like.

As I sat in the first row of the balcony, looking down at the action on the House floor, it was magical. In the face of the ridiculous amendments and only slightly concealed bigotry on display, watching the bill's House sponsor, Rep. Melanie George, refute some of the opposition rhetoric was like watching Gregory Peck as Atticus Finch in the film *To Kill a Mocking Bird* make a plea for 1930s-era civil rights.

From the ornate state house surroundings to the heat in the balcony and our rapt attention to the speakers on the floor below, the moment mirrored Atticus Finch's courthouse stand. With the balcony filled almost 100 percent by gay and gay friendly supporters, the scene also echoed that film as the discriminated against parties listened to their ally, Rep. George, eloquently speak out for doing the right thing. And, yes, it was so hot up there we were fanning ourselves, just like in the film.

When, just one week after the bill cleared the State Senate and after hours of often painful-to-hear debate, the bill passed 26-15, the balcony and floor below erupted in cheers and tears, with supporters hugging each other, most smiling, some sobbing, as discrimination in Delaware took it on the chin.

The photographers aimed their lenses toward the balcony to get the crowd reaction and the photos appeared on front pages all over Delaware. Then, they were picked up on the AP wire and showed up on the internet and in newspapers all over the country.

As luck would have it, the Nikons caught me in the delta between cheers and tears and friends all over the country saw a photo of me gape jawed like I'd been kissed by George W.

Bush. Never mind, it's the event that counts. Really, really counts.

Within minutes for some, hours and days for others, folks all over Delaware were being proposed to. "Will you civil union me?" It's a little longer than "Will you marry me?" but unless we're counting the cost of words for a skywriter to blow exhaust across the horizon, it makes no difference at all.

As for those dips in the euphoria, one came from a tragedy and one from a celebration. When a gay couples' home burned two weekends ago, the house and contents of the owner were insured but not the belongings of the same-sex partner—her name had never been added to the policy. Who knew??? A spouse would have been covered automatically.

The second detour was more subtle. A couple we know, having been married in all but name only for almost 30 years, laughingly announced their engagement in anticipation of a January civil union. The news was greeted quite seriously, with cheers and congratulations by their straight but not narrow friends and colleagues. And all that support felt really good.

But in a strange way, that their announcement was taken so seriously and so literally carried a little sting of insult. So many couples have been in an equivalent marriage for so, so long, and it felt a bit like those years were being negated.

Maybe I'm being a little overly defensive. After all, we can't help the reactions of straight people. It's not their fault. They were born that way and we love them equally anyway. It's not their fault they don't understand the nuance of our specific culture. We often don't understand theirs.

Besides, when all of us do start civil unioning in 2012, we certainly want the goodies that go with it. His and His towels, Hers and Hers bathrobes, and of course, new kitchen appliances. I sure hope local merchants set up civil union registries.

Thanks to our wonderful legislators and activists taking the lead on this, hold onto your hats caterers, beverage providers, DJs, etc....here come the civil unioneers. Yee-Haw!!!▼

Queer Camping in Sheville

For years this column has been called CAMPout for no specific reason except, I guess, a cutesy name for the CAMP Rehoboth magazine, and let's face it, I am out.

But lately, with our acquisition of an RV, things are changing. We appear to be CAMPingOut and oddly, after more than 15 years, this column is aptly titled.

And last month we camped out in Asheville, North Carolina, where I was invited to speak about lesbian publishing for the University of North Carolina Queer Conference. Did you gulp at the phrase Queer Conference? I did. I know gay kids are reclaiming the word queer, but to tell the truth it still gives me the yips.

However, there I was, and this column is about queer things ("adj. odd from a conventional viewpoint"), like this author passing up the conference rate at a Four Seasons for a campsite.

We drove in the RV, towing the Tracker, down the Eastern Shore of Virginia (Yay, Temperanceville!) across the foggy, rainy Chesapeake Bay Bridge-Tunnel (what scenic view?), through a thick slab of Virginia, into North Carolina, turned right and headed across the state.

A pea soup fog descended as we threaded our way up Black Mountain, past the Eastern Continental Divide—which I determined to mean you couldn't see a thing in either direction for an equal distance from sea to shining sea.

Bonnie at the wheel, Fay with her laptop Schnauzers, made the ten hour trip, forgoing attractive temptations like the Daniel Boone Family Festival, a roadside gun show, the museum of tobacco, and the plethora of convenience stores flying the confederate flag.

Obeying our GPS, we turned left at the sign boasting camping/prison facilities. Not encouraging. Then we saw

MapQuest warning, "You've gone a little too far if you get to Banjo Lane." They had to be kidding, right? Or should I be, as Ms. GPS said, recalculating?

So we turned, saw the campground sign, and began a chug straight up a perilously steep incline on a skinny, hairpin turn-strewn road, with sheer drop-offs on either side. Depending on your point of view, the posted signs, either snarky or encouraging, kept us going through the terror with phrases like "You can do it," "Just a bit further," and my favorite. "You made it!"

Frankly, I almost did. In my pants.

But once at our site we couldn't believe our eyes—a stunning vista to the valley below and more mountains across the way. A flock of wild turkeys greeted us, strutting around the RV with their tails fanned out, like colorful paper cutouts for Thanksgiving table centerpieces.

One look at a lunging Schnauzer and the birds showed us the origins of the phrase turkey trot. And then, to our surprise, they took off in gorgeous flight…who knew? I'd heard that Ben Franklin wanted our national bird to be the turkey, and I always equated that idea with his ill-advised key and kite thing, but no, these turkeys were stunning in flight. I'm not so sure that adopting the turkey instead of our mean-spirited current national bird is wrong in these mean-spirited times.

I awoke in our comfy RV Friday morning, April 1, dressed for my panel appearance, and ventured outside to find a lacey dusting of snow. April Fool, indeed. I navigated the car, carefully, very carefully down the ski-slope mountain, to the school.

I have to say it was a little jarring to pull onto campus and see big signs announcing "Queer Conference This Way." The program of speakers and topics just floored me. Hundreds of students and visitors signed up to attend this great big gay conference, with people filing into the registration area, acting as if it were no big deal.

But for me, it was a big deal. When I was in college people smoked grass in the open but whispered the word lesbian in the closet—and nobody majored in it, socially or academically. Holy Hasheesh, look what 40 years can do. It's queer, it's here and apparently this whole campus is used to it.

My conference packet included a dashboard parking permit with four inch letters shouting QUEER CONFERENCE! I looked back at my car with its proud windshield declaration and laughed, recalling, for some reason, my first drive to a gay bar.

I'd parked my brand new 1979 vehicle in a dicey DC neighborhood, preparing to slink to the bar. I panicked upon realizing that my vanity license plate spelled Fay J. Furtively, I took a t-shirt from the car and draped the license plate in a self-loathing shroud. And I was 31 years old at the time.

Today, the students walked into this conference holding hands, sporting pink hair, piercings, leather leggings, and all manner of funky out-of-the-closet attitude. But the best part was that they were really smart, curious, and thrilled to be learning about all things literarily Queer (see, I'm getting used to the word).

Well, I had a blast. In addition to the academic endeavors, we saw wonderful comic Jennie McNulty perform, had an evening at an eclectic downtown bar called Tressa's (the ethnic mix and combo of gay and straight rocked), and I learned that Asheville is often spelled with the first A dropped, as in SHEVILLE. It seems it's a fantastic city for lesbians. Much as Rehoboth sports a mighty contingent of lesbian retirees, Sheville has the younger ones. It stands to reason, as it's a city, and there are real jobs there.

We were sad to say goodbye to our weekend home, leaving our turkey friends behind and rolling up and down the rolling hills toward home. At least we thought we were going home. I pushed the button for home on the GPS and about ten minutes down the road saw the sign Welcome to Tennessee. Recalculating? Hope the bitch on the dashboard didn't think we said Dollywood instead of Delaware.

Turns out we took a new route, through true banjo territory, toward Virginia and home. We did not stop to buy fireworks, attend one of a dozen mega-church Sunday gatherings, or purchase Raw Peanuts along the roadside.

But it was all very queer, as in "adj, odd from my conventional viewpoint." I loved it. Camping OUT, wild turkeys, mountainsides, queer conferences, and all. Even at my age, I'm recalculating.▼

May 2011

May 11: As I write this, it's National Eat What You Want Day. Honest. It was on the internet. For me, however, there shall be no celebrating this calendar creators' phony holiday.

I've got a stomach ulcer, and I'm surprised. I'd always thought of myself as a carrier, giving others roiling stomachs. But no, for some reason my system has rebelled. I am gobbling antacids and staring at a medical version of the NO FLY list. In this case it's the NO EAT list.

That I've been warned away from all coffee, alcohol and spicy or fried foods, (did I mention alcohol?) two days before I leave for New Orleans is as cruel a twist of fate as I can remember. The good news is that on this, my seventh annual trek to NOLA, I may be able to recall, for the first time, what I did and who I met.

May 12: Off we fly to my annual Saints and Sinners LGBT literary festival, choosing saint rather than sinnerhood when offered a cocktail on the plane. While gastric issues partly motivated my decision, saving a few bucks was key, too. I'd already paid an extra $20 for my suitcase's plane ticket. And by the time we checked in, there were only middle seats left, so Bonnie and I each paid another $20 to sit together in an exit row with more leg room.

"You are in the exit row, ma'am, are you willing and able, in case of emergency, to remove the heavy exit door and place it on your seat?"

"Yes," I said. Frankly, I would like to remove the heavy exit door and place it on top of the AirTran CEO.

After checking into our Big Easy hotel we went directly to the Acme Oyster House, where dinner was big but not easy on the stomach lining. Gumbo. Fried Shrimp Po' Boy. Abita beer. Hopefully my doctor does not read this magazine. I won't tell him that I fell off the ulcer wagon twenty minutes in. But I had a theory. If I could keep my stomach full, the spice and alcohol would hurt less. Rationalization is such a gift.

So it did actually turn out to be Eat Anything You Want Weekend. The ulcer diet could kick in Monday.

May 13: First thing: Café Du Monde for beignets and chicory café au lait. I hoped the au lait would protect my stomach from the au coffee.

From breakfast I went to a master class given by social networking and promotion guru Michele Karlsberg. With a barrage of terms, from tweeting, tagging, and widgets to blog tours, RSS feeds and embedded buttons, the whole thing gave me the vapors. By the end, the only thing I learned for certain was if I wanted to do this stuff I had to hire the teacher to do it for me.

By mid-day, in this city where you can walk in the streets with a drink in your hand and there are food choices every-where, I learned something. If I ate every two hours, I could keep the belly pain at bay. It was tough, but oh po' boy did I manage! The jambalaya lunch with a mid-afternoon hush puppy chaser did the trick. I bet you're not surprised to learn that on Decatur Street, lamp posts have little cocktail shelves attached so you can hang out, sipping Hurricanes and listening to street entertainers. From washboard bands to big "second line" jazz combos, as long as you are upright and have a to-go cup the night is young.

Sadly, I am not. There was only so much I could take before heading back to the hotel for a nightcap of Tums Smoothies and Nexium.

May 14: It's a conspiracy. They served complimentary mimosas at the morning conference sessions. I asked for plain champagne. Alcohol I can handle; it's the orange juice that will kill me. While my spouse was off on a swamp tour I was happily alligator-free at the conference sessions.

I was delighted to be asked to sit on a memoir panel with some outstanding writers, including pioneering gay author Felice Picano and a delightful newly-published memoirist

Aaron Anson. But, lesbian theatre queen that I am, I was happiest sitting next to actor Bryan Batt (Sal on Mad Men, the original Darius in Jeffrey) who wrote a truly hilarious and moving memoir mostly about his mother, but with tales of growing up in New Orleans and his theatre career. He calls it a "Momoir" and, reading it on the flight home I laughed out loud, enjoying his honesty and heart. Read it. It's called *She Ain't Heavy, She's My Mother*. The man can act, sing, and write. Hardly seems fair.

To be honest, I was so flattered I was struck speechless when Felice Picano told me he thought the column I read was a terrific piece of writing. I'm still floating, but perhaps part of that is all the gumbo.

On Saturday late afternoon we went down to see the mighty Mississippi, mightier than usual with the portent of horrid flooding thundering toward the Bayou and New Orleans. Where in past years we could stand at our favorite spot near Café Du Monde and see the tops of ships passing by, this time we could see their hulls. The water was almost up to the riverside promenade and it was scary.

So we retreated from the waterfront and spent Saturday evening on Frenchman Street, an area with authentic live music by local musicians as opposed to the commercial touristo hoopla that is Bourbon Street. We stopped into several clubs, and I ate more verboten food and drank more prohibited cocktails. We ended the evening coming upon an outdoor wedding celebration at Jackson Square, complete with a New Orleans brass band and a sing-a-long with the wedding party and hundreds of strangers to "When the Saints Go Marching In." Quintessential New Orleans.

And the good news, at least for downtown New Orleans, was that by this time, the Corps of Engineers had opened the spillways and floodgates upstream, flooding the bayou, farm-land and tiny towns to save the cities. It was a Sophie's Choice, but one that needed to be made. It turned out that we had gotten to see the river at its most threatening that afternoon.

Sunday morning was for farewell beignets and chicory coffee, and I was dumb enough to wear black pants for a meal guaranteed to cover my clothes with powdered sugar. If anybody in the restaurant so much as sneezes, it looks like a white Christmas in there.

On the ride to the airport, our wonderful cab driver was worried about his home in the bayou, expecting the spillway water to inundate his community. It made us sad, and reminded us that the delta has been terribly affected by global warming and things like this are going to continue to happen. We wished the cabbie well and tipped big.

So we're home now after a marvelous book event and an acidic food binge. I have sworn off all liquor, spicy food, coffee and other things bad for my stomach. Beignet, done that. Time to heal.▼

May 2011

It's getting to be bathing suit season, so I'm pumping iron. Again.

Up to now, I've been the kind of customer gyms like as I eagerly join and fork over my money. Now there's irony for you. If there hadn't been so many forks over I wouldn't have to do this at all. But my modus operandi is to pump iron for the first few weeks and thereafter get most of my exercise just writing a check for the monthly dues. Now, with online bill pay, even my wrist is flabby.

Once, back in the day, I bought a life-time gym membership, meaning I could drop out that year, the next year, and every year in perpetuity. As it turned out, the deal was for the gym's lifetime, and it was cut down in its prime.

Then, at a place called Spa Lady, I signed up for water aerobics.

"Ladies," said the instructor, "leap out of the water onto the side of the pool and using your arms pretend you are a seal. Honk and balance a ball on your nose." I felt like a walrus not a seal and almost drowned when I realized that the mirror was actually a picture window to the gym lobby. Orca the exhibitionist never went back.

Next, I joined a snazzy urban club, with high-tech apparatus. The hybrid rowing machine/video game talked. "Keep up, keep your back straight, pull through the entire stroke," droned a snarky robot while I struggled to keep up with the digital pace boat. "You are two boats behind," it warned. Stroke, stroke, I'm rowing away...and the news got worse "You are four boats behind." I kept rowing, ignoring the mounting tally of phantom vessels whizzing past.

"You are twenty-seven boats behind" the voice smirked, registering Calories Spent: 31. That's one bite of a Hostess Snowball. On my last stroke, praying I wasn't having one, I had an itch and removed a hand from the grab bar to scratch, capsizing myself onto the floor like a tanker in a squall. Getting my behind off the gym mat should have counted as my requisite squats.

One time, I was intercepted by a fitness counselor.

"Do you take your heart rate after rowing?" she asked.

"No."

"Don't you want to know if you've reached the cardio rate for burning fat?"

"No. Whatever my heart is doing while I'm losing the regatta is better than what my heart is doing when I'm watching Jeopardy and eating cheese doodles." She left me alone.

Then I tackled the weights. On my first day I could lift the equivalent of a box of Kleenex. In four weeks I worked my way up to the bulk of a bag of Dunkin' Donuts. It occurred to me I could just as easily do this for free at home.

Then my pal the fitness counselor walked by.

"Are you making progress?"

"I bought a work-out outfit." She left me alone.

So there I was, in my new Nike Just Do It T-shirt and evil elastic pants cut for Cher, not me, tackling a machine called the Gravitron. Invented by rocket scientists, the machine jacked me up like an old Studebaker and propelled me to do far more chin-ups than was wise.

As I was flung toward the ceiling, pumping myself up and down in a frenzy, I worried I'd sprout biceps like Conan the Barbarian. I also realized that the waif who installed me on the machine didn't discuss disengagement. I got off before becoming Popeye, but I should have had them foam the runway.

A week later, my progress mentor spied me again.

"How are we doing?" she asked.

"I bought an iPod." She left me alone.

And before I could go back the following week and show off my new finger-tip-less work-out gloves, this gym, too, expired.

Better it than me, I said. And by this time I was living at the beach and starting to realize the value of exercise. Wanting to get in shape and, come bathing suit season, not frighten the tourists, I had a fleeting flirtation with yoga and did some power walking.

I've tried boardwalking (early morning, before funnel cakes and fries are born), peddling my home exercycle/towel rack, mornings at Curves, evenings at aerobics and all manner of other ultimately unsuccessful work-out regimens. I'd attempt running but I know my only strength in that arena is running my mouth.

But just when I feared that last season's clothes were thrift shop bound, I heard of a group of my peers working out three mornings a week. I up and joined them. No fancy video machines, no Disney rides, no trendy exercise accessories but a small room with recumbent bikes, weights, and a versatile machine for crunches and leg presses.

Oh, and on that piece of equipment I can stretch my legs out, pull at a bar tied to an upright and be on the rowing crew again. I'm actually having fun. It's amazing how much better I do without a digital jerk warning there's a coxswain creeping up my butt.

And I certainly don't miss orbiting on a Gravitron, chins flapping from the G-force or doing pool tricks like Shamu the Whale.

I'm lifting weights, stretching, laughing a lot and checking my heart rate. No lifetime membership needed. Is happy a heart rate? Pumping irony. I think I finally feel the burn. ▼

SOMEBODY STOLE MY DONUT...

I feel it's only fair to let all my readers know exactly how clueless, unbutch, and ignorant I am when it comes to motor vehicles.

Perhaps it was the poster I once saw on New York's Christopher Street that said, "If it has tires or balls, you're going to have trouble with it."

Maybe that sentiment steered me away from cars and toward the lavender brick road, who knows. But in any case, this story involves a donut, and not the jelly kind. The donut in question is the kind nestled in the trunk of your car in case of a flat tire. I learned the term some time ago as we suffered a blowout in the boonies of Delaware. Smyrna. Where it happened is not germane to this story but I love the name Smyrna.

Anyway, I learned of my donut ownership from my spouse who was cursing a blue streak and heading to the trunk for the aforementioned cute-looking little mini-tire for use just as far as the nearest gas station. But I guess that you, unlike me, already knew that.

So, one morning a couple of weeks ago I came out to the garage...let me rephrase that...I went out to the garage. I didn't need to come out to the garage. It already knows I'm a lesbian who doesn't know my carburetor from a frou-frou valve.

So I went out to the garage and found a flat tire. At this point I will tell you I had a friend with me, whose name I shall not mention lest everybody know that she didn't fare so well in donut 101 either. You see, I opened the trunk, lifted the protective mat and saw what looked to me like a donut hole without a donut in it.

"My donut is missing! Somebody stole my donut!" I sputtered, accusing some poor mechanic or desperate donut-less schnook of pilfering my baby spare. "What do I do, put out an APB on my donut?"

To her discredit, my pal looked into the trunk and, said, "Oh my gosh," alluding to the fact that she, too, didn't see any damn donut.

By my second, "Somebody stole my donut," we both started to giggle because that statement sounded so stupid. Little did we know exactly how stupid. Mistake one. I did not call my spouse. I handled the mechanical crisis myself—never a good move. I called roadside assistance which immediately sent a tow truck. They should have just sent me a real lesbian.

Dumb and dumber show up with their tow truck and when I tell them my donut us missing, they peek in my trunk and verify that fact. I think they just took my word for it so they could wrap this up and go get an actual donut.

"No problem," said one of the brain trust mechanics, further validating my conclusion about the errant donut. "Let's pump up the tire, see if it holds the air, and we will follow you to the tire store."

Which is exactly what happened. Whereupon they waved bye-bye, I learned that the tire valve stem thingie, was leaking, I bought a new one for $15—clearly the cheapest repair ever, and went on my merry way. Oh, except for feeling quite violated and telling everybody who would listen that somebody had pilfered my donut.

Then, like a schmuck, I put the tale on Facebook. Ha-ha funny story, ha-ha somebody stole my donut. By the next day, one of my pals came by with a donut spare she got at a yard sale, another showed up with a rusty but serviceable donut, and a third generous but snarky friend brought me an actual dozen Krispy Kremes.

Enter my friend, the gayboy car guru. He stops by my house, gets out of his truck, wordlessly goes over to my car, pops the trunk and unscrews the wing nut in the donut hole, opens the plastic cover and reveals, ta-da, my donut.

Who feels like a wing nut now?

I had to issue a mass mea culpa for the false accusations of a donut heist. Repercussions resulted.

FB friend: "Hey, Fay, make sure you put "summer" air in those tires…you don't want to be driving around with "winter" air in them now.

FB friend: Check your muffler bearings, too"

FB friend: "Don't forget to change your turn signal fluid."

Me: "Go ahead, have your little fun, I deserve this."

Gayboy car guru: "I out butched Fay Jacobs."

Me: "That's not hard."

FB friend: "How can a gay man know more about cars than a lesbian?"

Gayboy car guru: "I know my way around a car, truck or any other vehicle! I also know every isle of Home Depot, Lowes and I have power tools! I like sports and I can fix things too!"

FB friend: "That's not the issue. Why doesn't Fay know these things?

Gayboy car guru: "That part of Fay's brain is filled with show tunes. This is all part of our own diversity. Oh by the way, not a show tune fan here and get ready to take my card away; I hated Rent!"

Me: "So much for stereotypes. I wouldn't know what to do with a jumper cable if you put a revolver to my head."

Gayboy car guru: "Okay, sung like Ethel Murmon, 'There's no business like the car business like…'"

Me: "Oy, it's spelled Merman. Hand over your gay boy card please and I'll give up my lesbian cred."

So I'm outed as a mechanically ignorant gay girl and he's outed as a musical comedy dunce. Diversity is alive and well in the gay community and I love it. But with donuts on my mind, I now crave some Boston Cremes, If it's got tires or balls or carbohydrates I'm going to have trouble with it. ▼

June 2011

AFTER INTERCOURSE COMES PARADISE

On the first weekend of this month we revved up the RV and headed to Pennsylvania Dutch country to camp with a group called RVing Women. I'm sure nobody's shocked that all previous knowledge I had of the Amish came from the mostly-forgotten musical *Plain and Fancy* starring Barbara Cook.

It also won't shock you to know the weekend included Intercourse. No, it's not too much information. We're talking Intercourse, the town, here; any other kind will not be mentioned. Frankly, the only naughty thing I did all weekend was sit around a campfire and enjoy it.

We set out on Thursday with the Schnauzers and enough food and drink to feed and anesthetize the Israeli Army. After a couple of hours, amid an area littered with tattoo parlors, tractor supply stores and hog farms, we saw the sign. Paradise, 3 miles. I don't think so.

But a mile on the other side of the self-proclaimed town of Paradise we found our destination—the Old Mill Stream Campground. Literally, down by the old mill stream, we hooked up the RV to electric, water, and sewer and went exploring.

In the campground pavilion, I found the leaders of this RVing Women troupe—the Mid-Atlantic Chapter of a national organization—preparing food and activities for the weekend. We got a hearty welcome and saw that they'd scheduled a book reading and signing for me on Saturday. Would I survive until Saturday without Friday night happy hour in Rehoboth and with only outdoor activities to entertain me?

There were at least 30 rigs, some smaller than ours, but many waaaay larger, and they were all piloted by women, many with partners, and most with pups. Moxie and Paddy got to meet Lady and Pepper, two lithe female greyhounds. They also socialized with a charming boxer, several bichons, a

Toto-look-alike and numerous mutts, They all brought their humans with them, plus a bounty of booze and munchies. No fear of starvation between the three daily pot luck buffets.

For a woman out of her natural habitat, I adapted well. We sat around a campfire, a sprinkling of women in chairs, many on the turf, and a sprinkling of dogs on the turf, but many of them in chairs. I feared being made to sing Kumbaya, but frankly we talked politics and gay history. I was in my element again if you discount the embers and mosquitoes.

The reading and signing was a blast and on a walk up the road, we made the very rustic discovery of the Outlet Mall, which we happily avoided in favor of a game of redneck horse-shoes. What's happening to me???

Some women played Pickle Ball, a combination of tennis, ping-pong, and delicatessen. But the action stopped with the arrival of the Amish Pie Man, his horse pulling the wagon, his wife handling the transactions, and his pies beckoning us all. As we chomped down on our goodies I fully understood the origins of the name Shoo-fly Pie. (Sing it with me: Down by the old mill stream, where I first ate shoo.)

One great thing about these RVing Women—if you need assistance, look out. Somebody said, "Let's start a fire," and a woman came bounding out with an ax. While Lizzie Borden split logs like Abe Lincoln, other gals dispensed RV lore. We had twelve women with tool holsters offering opinions and a bunch willing to slither under anybody's rig and check for whatever might be ailing. Wow, that sounds naughty, too, but I'm really just talking about load levelers and pump-outs. Although after the dinner buffet I think I needed a personal load leveler.

For sheer contrast, our lesbian mechanical crew stood on one side of the old mill stream (had to say it again) and on the other side, an Amish farmer tilled his field with a plow drawn by a pair or horses. I'm sure if he had needed help, our women with axes would gladly have leapt the stream to assist.

For this novice camper, the RVing Women put out the

welcome mat and gave us reason to join the group. They are organized, they can cook, they encourage traveling canines, and they have a wealth of RV info and stories...and they don't even mind when somebody asks, "What kind of engine on your rig?" and I say, "the seats are beige."

By Sunday it was time to explore and naturally, I had to visit Intercourse, PA, and photograph the city limits sign. It wasn't easy. I walked to the side of the road, straddling a steep incline and side-stepping horse shit—and not the verbal kind I'm used to. An Amish family, spending Sunday on their porch, went inside while I did my photographic circus act. Bonnie said they didn't want to be in my picture but I think they didn't want us to see them laughing at the dumb tourist slipping in horse manure.

We traversed the countryside from Bird-in-Hand to Intercourse to Paradise, repeating the RVing Women mantra: "Not all who wander are lost." My personal adage is "Not all who RV wield an ax."

But I did wield the GPS, making certain we avoided taking the RV through any of the 28 covered bridges in the county. That would have been ugly. And everywhere we went, we wound up behind a horse and buggy with the "slow moving farm vehicle" red triangle on the back.

By the time we finished up the Amish bakery items and campfire cocktails, I was a slow moving farm vehicle myself, needing a butt triangle and load levelers. I'm an RVer and I like it. Go figure.▼

June 2011
Sweating It Out for Marriage Equality

Between Delaware celebrating the passage of Civil Unions and the stunning late-night vote to approve marriage equality in New York, it seems we're queer, we're here, and we're registering at Crate and Barrel.

That's the royal "we" of course, since Bonnie and I were married back in 2003 in Canada and now Delaware, along with New York and seven other states, will recognize our Canadian same-sex nuptials.

New York's vote was made all the sweeter as Bonnie and I traveled in the RV to a home by the Chesapeake Bay Bridge last weekend to celebrate with pride, the DC wedding of two very dear, longtime friends—and it was just as New York was heading up the vote.

But the gay pride we felt was only barely more than the personal pride I felt surviving this particular camping experience. It was my outward bound, kids, and, as I am fond of saying, bad decisions often make good stories.

The decision was to stay overnight in the RV on the bridal party's driveway the night before the wedding reception and the night of the party itself. Okay, on its own, it wasn't a bad decision, given the expectation of two days and nights of eating, drinking, and dancing. So the devil, they say, was in the details of powering up the camper.

On Friday, after pre-wedding dinner and dancing, as I closely monitored the New York Senate marriage equality vote on my smart phone, its battery gave out, making it a dumb phone in every way. So, we said our goodnights and headed to the RV, where I could plug in the Droid and follow up our live pre-wedding party with the virtual New York gay wedding watch.

But alas, a second RV was on site as well, and with both of us plugged into the same garage electric circuit, disaster struck. Minutes after we staggered back to the creature comforts of The Bookmobile, the circuit blew, plunging us into total darkness. Minus the air-conditioner, the RV soon became a pitch-black Native American sweat lodge.

"Crap, even Motel 6 leaves a light on for you. God, it's dark in here," I said, "and no guide dogs. But I'm glad they're with the dog sitter, not suffocating with us." As I lay frying, indeed. No air, no light, no marriage equality updates.

"We'll be okay," Bonnie said, "it will cool off soon. But let's sleep with our heads at the foot of the bed where there's more air circulating."

As we reclined, about-face, panting and sweating, a miracle happened, and we drifted off to sleep, aided, perhaps, by three hours of champagne toasts.

Suddenly, Bonnie let out a honking snort of a snore, I scooted over to smack her, but being upside down on the bed, I went the wrong way and fell off, wedging myself between the bed and the wall.

"What the hell???" hollered Bonnie, jolted awake by the thump and the expletives. She turned to find me, and likewise, went east, not west, plunging off the other side of the bed. Now we're both between a rock and a hard place on opposite sides of the bed and of course, starting to laugh.

But it was searing hot in the vehicle and we were desperate. So, getting back to her feet, Bonnie feels her way by Braille, inching to the control panel to turn on the battery operated fans. Who cares if the batteries die and the rig won't start tomorrow. It won't matter if we suffocate tonight. I reach out to guide her back to bed promptly poking her in her eye, and while she's flailing and shouting "Ow," she crashes into my knee caps and we're now back in a pile on the floor, still laughing.

Back in bed, air starting to move a little, we drift off—and then we hear it: a beep like a smoke detector. Beep. Beep. Beep.

Me: "Jeez, now what?"

"It's that thing on the wall," Bonnie says, presumably pointing to the tiny red light blinking on the plastic device at the head of the bed. I inch toward it on my hands and knees, put my face up to the meter, with one eye trying to read the words by the glow of the blinking, beeping red light. The largest letters say "Replace by 2006." Oh, goody.

Me: "I can't see this thing, shit, it's like the bottom line on the eye chart. Nobody our age can read this. Wait, wait, oh for god's sake, it's in French. It says defaults...oh, here's the English, F-A-U-L-T. It says fault."

Bonnie: "Fault? What does that mean?"

Me: "It means it's your fault. This whole camping thing is your fault. Why did you ever think I could adapt to living like this? Jews don't camp."

So the two of us are laughing again and have to pee, and it's anybody's guess where the door to the bathroom is.

Finally, Bonnie deduces that the blinking light means low voltage and the vehicle battery is dying. At which point the fans sputter and stop. "I don't hear you laughing," Bonnie says as the place began to heat up again.

"When's the ceremonial purification rite? If I wanted a sauna I would have joined a health club. I'm simmering here."

"Don't worry," says my sweat lodge director, "I'll turn the engine on and it will charge the battery and get some air-conditioning going."

"Well, you'd better, or at least baste me and cover me with foil."

So she did, turn the engine on, that is, then fell promptly back to sleep.

Life is cruel. I finally got rid of the hot flashes and night sweats and here I am, living the dream again. Meanwhile, Bonnie is snoring away while I lay wide awake worrying we're being asphyxiated by engine exhaust.

I didn't have to fret long. The beeping started and Bonnie shot up and rolled right back onto the floor. This time it was another kind of warning beep, probably alerting us to carbon monoxide poisoning. So we turned off the motor, the beeping stopped and the place turned back into an E-Z Bake Oven. I was waiting for the Butterball turkey button to pop on my belly when we finally decided to get dressed and just wait for sunrise.

Staggering, sweaty and sleepless, out of the RV, we discovered that where there were once two RVs plugged into the electric, our cord was no longer in the socket. The occupants of the RV next to us on the driveway must have investigated the earlier blown circuit, tripped it back, unplugged our rig and left theirs attached for a great night's sleep with air and light.

Grrrrrrr. I had to be restrained from banging on their windows.

But pretty soon the sun rose and so did some of the guests from the house. We learned that the NY vote was a yea (yay!), had a grand time at the wedding party, and then, by nightfall, the other rig pulled out and we had the all-important electric circuit all to ourselves. Now that is my kind of circuit party— celebrating marriage equality and luxury camping.

Those are the important things. I'm not sweating the small stuff. ▼

SOMETIMES YOU GET A WAKE-UP CALL

I apologize in advance, because this column is not going to be the least bit funny.

It's about shock, sadness, some understandable complacency, perhaps a premature victory lap and the specter of a man riding around with a white sheet on his head.

The phone rang several hours ago and a man asked for me by name.

"I'm Fay Jacobs," I said.

He asked if I was the one who wrote the letter to the editor using the term "traditional family values" being code for anti-gay. It was the letter about the Mayor, he said.

I knew exactly what letter it was. It was one in which I expressed disappointment that in the *Washington Blade*, Rehoboth's Mayor Cooper was quoted as wanting to keep "establishments from spoiling Rehoboth's status and tradition as a family-oriented vacation destination." I don't even think the Mayor meant it as anti-gay. I think it was meant to express his concern about loud music and noisy bars. But I did want to make the point that "family-oriented" is often used as code for anti-gay and we should be past having the Mayor use the coded phrase, however inadvertently, when discussing Rehoboth Beach.

I told the caller that I wrote that letter, and he began explaining, rather quietly, that I was an enemy of the United States for pushing the homosexual agenda, demeaning the tradition of one man and one woman and how dare I demean family values.

"You are a disgusting person who, along with all the homosexuals in town, ruined Rehoboth Beach. I am going to do everything within my power to protect my children from the likes of you and those disgusting homosexuals in Rehoboth, even the ones who think that they have won their rights and convinced some politicians to put forth the dangerous homosexual agenda."

I was so stunned I couldn't even hang up. I quietly asked him his name and, of course, he refused to give it to me, and continued with his scary, quiet conversation that so frightened me I almost threw up.

I asked if he lived here and he intimated that he did. He just kept talking and I don't remember much of what else he said, because I was numb.

I asked him why, since I was proud to share my views in a public forum like a "Letters to the Editor" column, he did not answer my letter with his own views, attributed to him, in the newspaper. He told me he just wanted to talk to me personally so I would understand that this will not be tolerated. I told him that calling anonymously was cowardice.

I also told him I felt very sad that his gay neighbors frightened him so badly that he had to seek me out on the phone to call me names anonymously and denigrate me and so many, many other Rehoboth residents as well.

He protested that he wasn't frightened and I shouldn't think that gay people in Rehoboth have gotten away with anything—that there are people out there that won't let this town be destroyed by sick homosexuals and that we should all seek therapy and try to change. You are an enemy of the United States, he repeated, and you will not win, he was very, very quietly threatening. I said I was sad that he didn't value and learn from the diversity around him, and hung up.

We couldn't get a *69 number as he was a "private caller." Of course he was.

I called CAMP Rehoboth's Executive Director Steve Elkins and told him what had happened. He was horribly upset as well, counseling that if the man called again, it might be considered stalking, and the police might be able to trace the call. Steve told me that in all the years he has been a public figure with CAMP, he has never had a phone call like that. Anonymous letters, yes, but not a call.

I'd never received anything like this either, even with my more than 20 years as an openly gay writer and gay rights advocate.

So I called the police and reported the incident. The State Trooper I spoke with was very saddened to hear the story and sympathetic, but of course, we both knew there was nothing to be done. The anonymous call itself was not any kind of a crime. Further calls might be considered harassment or stalking and the officer gave me a case number should I hear from the man again. He figured I would not.

Needless to say, the incident set me and Bonnie on edge and ruined the night. But it told me a few important things: First, like Klansmen riding around in their hoods, there are people here who have to hide while spreading their vicious hatred.

Second, some of us, myself included, might be a little too complacent about our freedoms here. It reminded me why CAMP Rehoboth was formed in the first place and why it is so important for CAMP to continue sensitivity training programs, outreach to the greater community, and efforts to make friends and stop bullying, hate-speech, hate crimes and plain old bigotry. Dances and art shows are nice, but CAMP Rehoboth is so much more than the fun stuff.

And finally, this incident, rather than make me cower and hide, makes me more determined than ever to be out, proud and working for equality. There are so many gay people, along with our straight but not narrow allies, who live here, embrace Rehoboth's diversity, and know we are all better for it. ▼

July 2011

I was out last night and several people asked me how my publishing company was doing.

"Great!" I said. Then I thought about it. So I decided to write this column as a window into the world of small publishing.

This summer, A&M Books, landed two finalist spots for the ForeWord Reviews' Book of the Year Awards, and my book, *For Frying Out Loud* won in the humor category. I'm thrilled. Not only is the award from a field of thousands of independently published books, but it was in a mainstream, and not just LGBT, category. I love that.

While I'm amazed and honored that the only two books tiny A&M published this year have both been recognized, visions of sugar plum fairies and enormous book sales are not exactly dancing in my head.

It's like my mother's stock answer when, as she was arguing with me, I raised what I deemed to be a valid negotiating point.

"One thing has nothing to do with the other," she'd say. And after all these years, it seems Mom was right. One thing really has nothing to do with the other.

As A&M Books' publisher I run a teeny tiny independent publishing house (and, as you know, it really is my house). The garage is the Rehoboth book depository, my spouse is fulfillment manager, and my Schnauzers are security.

And, as many readers also know, A&M Books has quite a history. The original owners were Anyda Marchant and Muriel Crawford (hence, A&M). Anyda wrote early lesbian fiction under the name Sarah Aldridge and the women, along with another couple, started Naiad Press in 1973. It became the largest lesbian/feminist publishing house in the world.

In 1995 Anyda and Muriel left Naiad (which is since defunct) to form A&M Books. When these two brilliant and fun women passed away in 2005 (Anyda at 95, Muriel at 93) they left me A&M Books.

All fourteen Sarah Aldridge novels were still in print and still selling, and my first book *As I Lay Frying—a Rehoboth Beach Memoir*, was heading toward a second printing. A&M was on a roll.

However, the bank account I inherited had about $11 in it. Apparently, one thing had nothing to do with the other.

It's six years later and we got word last spring that our two 2010 books won their respective categories for Delaware Press Association Books of the Year. The winners were my latest book and *The Carousel*, a wonderful contemporary novel by Stefani Deoul. *The Carousel* also just won an IPPY (another independent publishers award) Bronze Medal for LGBT fiction. Fabulous!

In contrast, the A&M bank account is shamefully overdrawn. Once again, one thing has nothing to do with the other. Well, in this case, it might have. I overdrew the account with the check for the Awards ceremony.

Bank fees aside, I'm having a great ride. My first book is in its third printing, having sold about 6,000 copies. Books two and three are doing well. But there are staggering costs of small, small publishing.

No matter the freight, I don't mind shipping books to independent bookstores. I'm happy they are surviving. But Amazon is another story. It's bad enough to pay a couple of bucks each to print the books, but add priority rate postage and Amazon's diabolical habit of ordering one book each for four different warehouses, and it's appalling. Oh, I forgot the $1.14 for the padded envelope. I'm lucky I'm not writing from a padded cell. Amazon stats up, net worth down. One thing has nothing, etc.

So here I sit, two cars turning into rust buckets on the driveway and a garage stacked with towering pallets of books. I'm drowning in sell sheets, backorders, and bubble wrap. My den is my distribution center, with books four feet high and purchase orders, packing tape, and the ubiquitous bubble wrap filling every available crevasse. In the clutter I can easily lose a Schnauzer. Those Clean House reality show people would take one look and burst into tears.

So, all these awards and good reviews are a great reward. I love that Facebook, blogs, and web pages are lit up with colleagues from other, bigger independent publishers congratulating me along with their own nominated authors.

Equally lit up are the little flashing parenthesis around the numbers on my online bank statement, noting the A&M Books account deficit. Yes, yes, it seems that one thing may have something to do with the other after all.

So how's the book biz coming? I'm having a blast and sometimes all this fun costs more money than the press makes. But what the hell. It's like the classic circus sanitation worker who follows the elephants with a shovel. "Why do you do this dirty work," he's asked. You know the answer: "What? And give up show biz?"

For me, it's "What, and give up the book biz?" I'm committed to keep shoveling.

Looky here. I just got a purchase order from Amazon for a whopping seven books to be sent to four separate warehouse destinations. I'm going to have a martini now. One thing has absolutely nothing to do with the other. ▼

DON'T HASSLE ME, I'M LOCAL

Can I bitch?

I was driving on Rehoboth Avenue yesterday when the car in front of me screeched to a stop, punched his flashers and sat behind a car with its trunk flung open. Clearly a visitor. Now you and I, but obviously not the fellow in the double parked car, know that an open trunk is a sign of, well, an open trunk. And it often bears no relation to whether people are packing up to leave the parking space.

So the light is green, but nobody can go because this yutz is waiting in case a space opens up this millennium. Finally, after stowing strollers that look like steam rollers, kites, boogey boards, coolers and a little league team, car number one tries to pull out, but car number two is camped behind it with nowhere to go because cars me through ten are grid-locked. Amid the sonata for horns, everybody misses their dinner reservation. Sometimes I wonder if vacationers leave their brains and manners back home with the cat.

I love the Saturday Night Fights. People drive around, see a vacant parking space and drop off the frailest person in the car to stand in the spot until the vehicle can come back around the block to claim it. Naturally, in the interim, six football players in a steroid rage drive up in a Humvee, leaving grandma to defend her position. Trust me, chivalry is as dead as Richard Nixon.

I actually witnessed somebody almost run over a tween saving a spot for Daddy's Caddy. It's like Armageddon out there, with Category 6 screaming matches. Mind you, these are the same people who jog up and down the boardwalk and run 10ks. God forbid they'd have to walk a block and a half to buy taffy.

Our traffic circle on the way in and out of town is another crime scene. The circle actually works pretty well for anybody who reads the sign "Yield to traffic in circle." What part of IN CIRCLE don't they understand?

Cars race to the circle and play chicken with drivers coming around from their left, like a round of bumper cars. If drivers entering the circle do yield, they often don't know when to come out of their coma. Here's a tip. If there's room for two Budweiser trucks and a team of Clydesdales between you and the car coming around the circle, move it.

Conversely, some fool is IN the circle but sees a car approaching and stops to let it in. Like lemmings, every car downtown now floods the circle and the goofball who stopped can cancel his hotel reservation because he'll still be sitting there by morning. Chivalry is as dead as Herbert Hoover.

Of course, our visiting pedestrians can disrupt traffic brilliantly as well. Throngs of aggressive jaywalkers, pushing fleets of baby strollers leap into the streets whenever they feel like it, making the screech of tires as ubiquitous a summer sound as chirping sea gulls. Yesterday I saw a man holding a pizza box with the lid up, eating a slice as he tried to cross the road. Do you want a seeing eye dog with that pepperoni?

And what's with the befuddled curb huggers, forgetting that green means go and red means stay. Nightly, they do the "should I stay or should I go?" dance on the corner, with their choice bearing no relation to traffic signals. It's like whack-a-mole in the street, only nobody gets a stuffed bear.

Down here, on the sand behavior is even worse. I see people arriving in moving vans, setting up the Kennedy compound, with pop-up shelters, portable gazebos (with mesh ventilating panels) beach cabanas, collapsible tables and industrial sized coolers. I love the ad for the cabana with a zippered door, offering "to keep out the sun and the sand." If I wanted to keep out the sun and sand I'd be on a bar stool on Baltimore Avenue.

And then these homesteaders plop their village directly in front me, not five feet from my chair. Seriously people. 15-feet of sand is the demilitarized zone.

Have you seen the new 8-foot umbrellas that could shelter half of Haiti? One good gust and the things will be in Portugal. Oh, that's right, they come with anvils on the bottom to anchor them. And don't forget the laptop and video games. It's the beach, people, bring a towel, a hat and a book (preferably, mine).

And these same imbeciles have no concept that at some point, given that the moon revolves around the earth, the tide will come in. They always look so shocked and expect us to move back, or worse, welcome them into our family. Am I rude not to want strangers' butts scooting onto my towel?

And what's with those footballs that make noise? Tossing a pig skin I can understand, but one that whistles Dixie is just annoying.

And while time flies when you are having fun, sand flies when your kids run in flip flops around my head. Leaving the beach? Check which way the wind is blowing. I know you want to shake out your towel, but I don't need a complimentary dermabrasion. Well, maybe I do, but that should be my decision.

Look, I want you to enjoy your Hip Hop and Country Billy music, but stick it in your ear. Personally, I'd rather hear show tunes but you wouldn't want me to subject your posse to *Les Miz*, would you? And of course, do not feed the sea gulls. When you go home we're left with gulls dive bombing us like we're Tippi Hedren in *The Birds*.

And finally, the reason dogs are not allowed on our boardwalk during the summer (they are allowed in areas of the beach at the state park and for that I am grateful), is directly related to the lady with a fluffy poodle who read the No Dogs on Boardwalk sign and sashays onto the boardwalk anyway. A police officer sees her, and she says "I'll just hold her." He tries to be nice, smiles and looks the other way.

Then the woman puts Fifi down to make a Great Dane-sized deposit on the boards, leaving without picking it up. Chivalry is as dead as Rin Tin Tin.

Okay, I know my town owes a world of gratitude to our wonderful visitors, but look, it's 104 degrees out and I'm grumpy. I will now drag my little beach chair down to the water and try to cool off. Ahhhhh. There, there, I'm better now. Thanks for indulging me. And come to the beach. I know you'll behave. ▼

If global warming is not happening, I'm Nanook of the North. It's a 100-degree day in July and I am homeless. Not that I'm sleeping in a cardboard box in front of Walmart, but technically, for the week, I have no home.

For a combination of good reasons, my July vacation was moved to August, after I rented my house out for the July dates. So here I am, on a day with a 110 degree misery index, dehydration warnings, and Route One pavement-buckling, sitting in my RV encamped at the Steamboat Landing RV Park just a few miles from my occupied home.

Outside my rectangular aluminum shelter, roads are melting, steam rises from the sand, and you can charbroil a hamburger on the dashboard of my car. As we lay frying, indeed.

So we decided to have a bit of a staycation, venturing outside of Rehoboth just a bit, to see if it was cooler in the hinterlands.

For me, that's a little like going into The Forbidden Zone in *Planet of the Apes*. For over a decade, as I worked promoting downtown Rehoboth, I always felt a bit traitorous dining in Lewes or exploring the M-towns (Milford Millsboro Milton) which took me a decade to tell from one another in the first place. In fact, if I did grace Second Street in Lewes or Federal Street in Milton, somebody would invariably spy me and holler "Oh, I didn't know they ever let you out of Rehoboth, he-he-he." It was easier to stay downtown. Even having retired from my tourism work, old habits die hard.

But this week, with license to roam, I got to hot-foot it (literally, given the weather) around the area, including Lewes, its downtown, its Historical Society and the Saturday Farmer's Market. As somebody who never saw a tomato out of cellophane until I was 30, had no idea carrots grew in the ground, and rarely made anything myself except reservations, this was a revelation. I bought a giant tomato that was actually bright red and checked out the artisan cheese, which apparently is now an art form. Van Gogh sold me the most fabulous stilton.

But by far, my favorite diversion of the Staycation was the Delaware State Fair.

On the way to Harrington, wending our way past Cricket Hollow and McCauley Pond, we passed a funeral home with a flashing sign shouting, "Save the Date!" Really??? Now I'm sure it was announcing some kind of community bus trip or something, but I sure as heck didn't want to stick around to find out.

How can I sum up the Delaware State Fair experience? I have never seen so many t-shirts with Confederate flags, John Deere tractors or beer slogans on them in my life. A personal favorite: "On a Beer Day You Can Pee Forever."

I'm sure fair officials strategically bring everyone in through the miracle mile of junk food, which is where we headed first, sharing a staggering array of shish-kabobs, pulled pork, corn dogs, cheese fries and other health foods. I'm surprised the Midway didn't have an angiogram ride.

It was a good thing we ate first since after spending considerable time in the cow and swine barns, I was a vegetarian by the time I got out. At the goat pens I learned the origins of the phrase "butting heads," and over with the sheep I got to utter my idea of writer's humor: "I love ewe."

And the noise! I haven't heard such booing since *Spiderman* opened on Broadway. Between the bleating and baaaahhing I thought I was at a session of Congress. I struck up a conversation with a prize-winning Nubian Goat who seemed to be calling Faaaaaay.

Outside the barns we stood to listen to The Citizens' Hose Company of Smyrna. Here was this awesome marching band, big and brassy, pumping out patriotic songs by the tuba-full. What fun! Although, given the heat, I worried that the horn players might set their moustaches on fire. I stood by with a cold lemonade, just in case.

Over at the produce exhibit, there were home-grown, prize-winning spuds and a giant bell pepper that looked like Henry Kissinger. Cinderella and her posse could have ridden in the blue-ribbon pumpkin and I was endlessly fascinated by the array of frighteningly phallic zucchinis. Now that's a vegetable.

Add in the Hollywood Racing Pigs, the carnies shouting "Every time a prize!" and the giraffe at the petting zoo, the Fair theme of "Come be a kid again!" worked for me.

For a while. The old gray mare, not being what she used to be, wilted pretty fast in the heat. At about Beer:30 Fair time, we headed off to our ersatz home, the rectangular aluminum estate. And by morning, as we traversed the scorched earth to the camp store for ice, it was still like walking through a blow dryer. Then we got the call. Our renters were heading home a day early and we could reclaim our territory.

With the dashboard thermometer registering 106 degrees, and weekend forecasts promising more of the same, we stopped to buy a three-ring inflatable pool for the deck. No diving.

So there I sat, up to my belly button in cold water, adult beverage in hand. Be it ever so humbling there's no place like home. Although, I'm disappointed that we didn't get to Laurel's Mr. Pepper's Pumpkin Patch & Sorghum Maze. Well, there's always next year. ▼

LET THERE BE LIGHT

Without warning, 7:15 p.m., Monday, August 8, was the day the music died. And everything else electronic. We suffered a blackout.

What the heck? Was this an isolated incident to drive me insane or was this blackout community wide? Outside, our neighbors wandered about, also wondering what had stopped their lives in their tracks. A car pulled up, with friends reporting that all of Route One, from Lewes to Rehoboth, was blacked out, traffic running amok, cars playing chicken at darkened signals, horns honking and people cursing.

As the sun quickly set in the West, I panicked. My daily to-do list stood incomplete as Bonnie and I sat quietly in the living room, no hum from the fridge, no TV, no computer, no A/C, dishwasher and laundry mid-cycle, and of course, damn cell phone battery waning. I thought of Simon & Garfunkel. The Sounds of Silence. I didn't like it one bit.

Well, at first, it was a relaxing little break. Sitting, talking, laughing, enforced tranquility. I never realized the dog snored that loudly. But then it started getting really, really dark in the house, increasingly warm, a bit spooky, and on my very last nerve.

Channeling Audrey Hepburn in *Wait Until Dark*, I rose from my chair, and feeling the walls along the way, went to the bedroom closet to find the battery operated light/radio. Emergency preparedness tip: don't stash the emergency device in the darkest, most inaccessible crevice in the house.

Borrowing the Braille method to search for the apparatus, I rummaged through purses last used in 1987, discarded brassieres, and a surprising number of errant golf balls plopping off the shelf (ow, ow, ow). Of course, once located, the radio was without batteries. So I used the hand crank, swiveling my rotator cuff to kingdom come to produce five minutes of radio reception. And I only got our local conservative hate radio. I'd rather be in a news blackout.

Meanwhile, Bonnie felt her way to the kitchen, found matches and lit a candle. It had an aroma like a Creamsicle ice cream pop. Pretty soon the house was hotter, only a flicker lighter and smelled like a Good Humor truck had exploded.

Naturally, I started to get the DTs from electronics withdrawal. Couldn't check e-mail or Facebook. Couldn't use my dying smart phone, couldn't write my column, couldn't watch *The Closer* (auuggghhh!), couldn't do a damn thing but obsess over what I couldn't do. It was not my finest hour.

"We could play cards by candlelight," Bonnie said.

"You mean cards in your hand, not on the computer?"

"Or, we could go inside and, um, nap."

"Are you kidding? It's 96 degrees in here."

"Okay, well just sit there then."

So I did, wondering what my Facebook friends were saying, curious if I had e-mail, writing my column in my head. I got pen and paper and scribbled without being able to see, most likely scrawling six sentences atop each other, creating indecipherable hieroglyphics.

Proceeding to the powder room, I tripped over a Schnauzer who, in turn, tripped over another Schnauzer. It was like wide world of Schnauzer wrestling in here. Finally, I pawed my way to the kitchen for the phone book (remember those?). Between my senior eyesight and the creamsicle glow I felt like Mary Todd Lincoln proofing the Gettysburg Address.

So I staggered to the antique hard-wired phone and found a dial tone—no lighted dial, mind you, but at least a dial tone. I thought I knew where the numbers were, but first called an exterminator, then a disconnected number. I was verging on completely disconnected myself when I finally got through to Delmarva Power.

"We estimate service to be restored by 11. We are evaluating the outage in your area."

Evaluating? If they're still evaluating, how do they know

when the lights will come on? And what are they evaluating? How long it takes to remove a tractor trailer from a light pole? If Glen Campbell is still a lineman for the county? How many lesbians it takes to change a light bulb?

My mind wandered. How many lesbians does it take to change a light bulb? One to change the light, two to make organic, free range supper, three to process alternative solutions?

Hello darkness, my old friend, I've come to talk with you again. The vision softly creeping, creeped me out. Deadlines missed, communication cut off. I fidgeted, then cursed and finally, risked letting the cold out of the freezer by opening it for ice cubes. The martini provided only temporary refuge from my panic. My name is Fay Jacobs and I am an electric junkie.

That's it. 9:30 and all I can do is go to sleep. So I tried. But there will be no alarm, so what will wake me up? I lay there, wide-eyed, terrified I'd be late for something I wasn't prepared for anyway because I hadn't done my work on the computer. Insanity, thy name is Jacobs.

Then, all of a sudden, my eyes were stabbed by the flash of a neon light that split the night. It came from the hall. Then, I heard it. The air-conditioning. Ahhhhh. And Kyra Sedgwick whining from the TV (yaaay!), and I saw the delicious glow of the telephone number pad. (Wheee!) Everything in the house started blinking, including Bonnie, who had been asleep on the sofa.

And in the naked light I saw my life return to normal. But the vision that was planted in my brain still remains. Clearly, I hated the sounds of silence.

So right then and there, I vowed to cut down on my electronic dependence. I would take up Scrabble again and crosswords with a pencil. I would turn over a new leaf and it would be the pages of a paperback book, not an e-reader. No more Facebook dependence. I would make old fashioned phone calls. I would meet people face to face. I would be a recovering tech addict. I would counsel others. I would no longer fear the sounds of silence.

But, of course, I was curious. What caused the blackout leading to my great epiphany? I ramped up my computer, went to our local news site and discovered the following report:

"Delmarva Power officials report that the cause of the power outage that hit the Rehoboth area just after 7:30 p.m. and affected over 3800 customers was a dead squirrel found in a transformer box."

Clearly, Toto, we're not in Manhattan anymore. In fact, it appears we are just one squirrel away from Gregorian chants, number two pencils, and subsistence farming. Let there be light. Please.▼

August 2011

Have you seen me lately, running around like a Perdue chicken with my noggin cut off? That's me, frantic, clothes wrinkled, gray roots showing, flying around town getting my chores done so I can go to my home office and spend all day, every day, not reading, not writing, but social networking so I can sell books.

But today I had a flash that hit me like a pail of cold water, which, was actually refreshing because it was 106 degrees out. Nobody's buying books because they, too, have no time to sit and read or iron or get their roots dyed because they, too, are spending their entire lives social networking.

UNCLE!!! I cannot Facebook, Twitter, web page, Branch out, or LinkedIn one more time today. I'm having a nervous breakdown and all I can think of is how to describe it in 140 characters or less. I have become seriously unglued and the only cure, as my book publicist says is to "step away from the e-machine," which is funny because she instructed me to do all this stuff in the first place.

Frankly, I've been social networking for years, writing columns about my life and pretty much being an open book collected in three open books. But, unless there was a point to it, I never stooped to writing I had lox and bagel for lunch or my dog had the trots unless it was part and parcel of a larger, hopefully amusing, story.

The magnitude of social media messages I get daily about what people are eating, wearing, and sadly, eliminating, is stupefying. What books they are reading, of course, is important, but it is clear to me from the posting that nobody has time for that old fashioned trivial pursuit. Noooo. Now we are tweeting and twirping non-stop, damn the torpedoes full 4G ahead.

But, thankfully, I had life savers like ice-cold Yeungling and fabulous air conditioning blasting away as I sat, portable e-machine on my lap, in my cool RV, social networking like my life depended on it.

Remembering I was at a campground with a pool, I donned my bathing suit and ran over for a short dip but felt guilty. I'm the short dip. I should be working, networking, e-talking, net-blabbing and otherwise surfing for promotional opportunities, not dunking in this delicious pool. Frankly, what I really should be doing is surfing at the beach, which is where I live, after all, but I never see it because I am too busy surfing the freakin' net.

Look, I'm capable of creating great feelings of guilt for just about any reason. Hell, it's in my DNA. But even I know I have reached a new level of manufactured angst with this kind of guilt. Step away from the e-machine.

So I did. I went out to lunch (No, unlike tweeter freaks, I will not tell you what I ingested). Hell, I'm semi-retired for pity's sake and I'm guilty going out to lunch? Even chain-gangs get lunch.

But when I got back, I got yelled at. Not by my publicist, not by my boss (me), but by the graphic of an owl on the Hoot Suite program I use to tweet, twitter, blather, and blog.

"You have been inactive for over an hour. I was bored, so I decided to take a nap. Let me know when you get back."

Jeez, even cartoon owls get to nap. I haven't had time to nap since kindergarten. I considered not telling the owl I was back, but since I'd failed to tweet for an hour and a half I was afraid the web would put out an all-tweets bulletin on me, declaring me AWOL, MIA or otherwise having left the information highway.

When I pushed enter to refresh my screen, I could see my Facebook page. And, in the upper right corner was the oddest thing yet. Under the heading Friends You May Know, there was a profile picture of composer Stephen Sondheim, with a note saying You have eight mutual friends. Really? Eight degrees of separation between me and Stephen Sondheim?

I clicked on the mutual friends and found two people I

know who really might be actual friends of the Broadway legend, but six others who, like me, are merely drooling fans. No, I do not believe I should bother to "friend" my pal Stephen.

And that's where Facebook gets interesting. When I get a friend request from somebody whose profile says "you have 253 friends in common" I know it's probably another writer and our mutual readers. Fine. But when I get a request that says you have 12 friends in common, it might sound like a lot, but it's probably that you both frequent the same dry cleaner. I have so many Facebook friends for the book biz I no longer know who I actually know and who I virtually know. I admit it. I'm an e-mess.

Which brings me back to my original point. Am I'm destined for the Betty Ford Clinic for tweet addicts? Am I about to be committed for a third degree text offense? All this tweeting and blogging has got to stop. Or at least be put on hiatus. Which is why, as you read this, Bonnie and I have taken off in The Bookmobile for parts North, heading for a quiet, relaxed, cheap and easy vacation. I will allow myself about 45 minutes a day to report to you via the e-machine. Til then...I'm signing off. Over and out, real and virtual friends. The e-machinist has left the building. ▼

When my mate suggested we do a zip line through the trees in the White Mountains of New Hampshire, I knew it was way outside my comfort zone, but I had read the brochure. "Family fun. Ages 9 and up. A stunning view over the tree canopy."

How bad could it be? I don't know what I pictured. Maybe a starter zip, a zip line light, a mini-zip. I felt sure we'd be on the bunny slope of zip lines.

I was buttressed into my gear, complete with helmet and body harness, then lectured on safety by a Paul Bunyan-like 20-year old. Okay, there really were children getting outfitted and their parents weren't calling 911.

But when the instructor offered advice about controlling flight speed, reality bit. For me, was the "appropriate clothing" suggested by the brochure a diaper?

Nervous and weighed down by gear, I toddled off to the zip site. Then the guide said, "For the first zip we will launch from the ground."

FIRST?? I saw the enormity of my blunder.

The guides attached me and my industrial strength canvas harness to a block and tackle pulley system, on a cable between the ground and a teeny tiny platform on a tree a mile down the mountainside. I was about to zip into the next zip code.

"Stand on this boulder, crouch to a sitting position and gently push off," said Big Foot the guide. Great, I can't do squats at the gym and I'm supposed to squat on a rock? I felt like a Sumo wrestler trying for the lotus position.

"And if you feel yourself spinning right or left, simply turn into the spin, like a car turning into a skid in the snow." Crap. I never understood that concept.

I could feel the muscular guide's open hand on my back, gently suggesting it was time for me to slide my scrunched-up torso off the boulder and down over the trees.

Zippity-do-daaauuggghhh!!!

I hit the air, the harness locked to the cable and I was off, semi-squatting, screaming, arms in the air, hanging by my thighs and crotch. What part of the word zip didn't you understand, you moron? God, don't let me pee!

I started to spin, helpless to right myself, zipping backwards toward the tree platform. "Incoming! Incoming!" I howled, sure I'd wipe out the unfortunate mountain man poised to snag me.

Apparently there was a wood block rigged to stop my forward motion, which, when I hit it, sounded like a gunshot. But no such luck. Unshot, marginally alive, I was passed, like a sack of Idaho potatoes, from one athlete to another to get rigged for a second zip.

When my spouse landed on the platform behind me, I spat, "I'm going to kill you!" just as the guide instructed me to jump off.

I gaped at the tree tops below. I was supposed to leap into mid-air, trusting the skinny cable to keep me from free fall? I'd rather die than bungee jump. I can't even jump into a swimming pool for pity's sake, much less sky dive! What am I doing here?

"I can't do this," I muttered.

"You have to," said Sasquatch. "There's no other way down."

By this time, zippers were piling up behind me as I stared, paralyzed, into the void.

"But I can't...Auuggghhh!!!!" Jumped or pushed? We'll never know.

What beautiful tree canopy??? With my eyes shut I could have been zipping over the county dump. And it's funny about gravity. The featherweight nine year olds had time to look around, but this big broad came zipping down the line like a freakin' space shuttle.

Zooming into the next outpost, hands in a death grip at the harness holds, praying I wouldn't kill anybody, I wound up suspended in midair, swinging like a fresh side of beef. I mouthed, "I'm going to kill you" to my mate, who appeared, dangling behind me, refusing to make eye contact.

Mentally, I filed for divorce as I was once again shuttled between a gaggle of outdoorsmen, who unclipped my cables, re-clipped me to other cables and hinged me to the zip line. Had anyone ever become unhinged? Physically, I mean. I was already mentally unhinged.

"Get ready for Zip Three!" yelled a bulky teenage guide, who suddenly grabbed me and tightened my harness so thoroughly I wanted to ask if he'd at least buy me dinner first.

"Off you go!" he hollered, sending me down the mountain at lightning speed. This time I faced forward, and, picking up speed, screamed "Cowabunga!" hoping not to have a coronary. I opened one eye to see trees flying by and a look of terror on the face of the poor schnook waiting to break my fall.

Thud! I practically flattened him, but he kept us both upright and rigged me for zip four. As I clenched my eyes and prepared for takeoff, I heard him say to the person I was formerly married to, "Things are getting better. This time she didn't say she was going to kill you."

Okay, so I came shrieking in for yet another klutzy crash landing, then had myself shackled and lashed to the line for the final zip. This time, the ride was tricky. I zipped down, then, by gravity, zipped up because the line stretched back up to a high tree. From there, gravity sent me down again, like a skateboarder on a half-pipe, not that I'd know from experience. I zipped back up and down two more times like Cirque du Soleil before settling in the middle of the cable, hanging like a pair of underpants on a clothes line. That's so they could yell "smile!" and take a picture.

When they got a ladder to offload me, my legs were rubber, my arms felt like lead, and even my hair was clenched. But I was happy to be on the ground, not in it.

"Well, what did you think?" ventured my spouse. "Are you proud you did it?"

Truth is, yes, I was proud. Quite pleased with myself, actually. And at least New Hampshire's motto, Live Free or Die, was not put to the test. And I guess I don't need a cardiac stress test. Been there, done that. Cowabunga.▼

September 2011

BRING ON THE LOCUSTS...

Let's face it, vacations are rejuvenating. Unless you're away from home during the historic trifecta of environmental events when Rehoboth gets an earthquake, tornado, and hurricane. As a writer, it's the pits to be out of town, out of touch, and missing the action.

Luckily, there was not that much action. The earthquake was but a tremble, the hurricane, thankfully, a no-show, and the tornado, while scaring many, mercifully produced no injuries and only property damage. All in all, not bad.

At word of the earthquake I was in a campground in Ogunquit, ME. We felt nary a shiver. Had I been home, I'm sure I would have run out into the street like Jeannette McDonald in *San Francisco*, shrieking and singing (although in her case, they were one and the same) "Nearer My God to Thee."

When we got news of impending Hurricane Irene, though, Bonnie decided we should head home a few days early to batten our hatches. When I whined, she suggested I batten my hatch and think about the six foot fiberglass dolphin on our stoop that could become airborne. Not to mention the gnomes in our kitsch garden.

So the traveling circus, me and Bon, the pups, the RV and the Jeep in tow, lumbered home down I-95 just in time to hear that Reho was being evacuated. Great. With thousands of cars pouring outbound on Route One, this was no time for us to be driving the Hindenburg head-on into the mess.

Quandary. Is there an insane pal along the route willing to harbor us, our dogs, and our rolling house for a four-day minimum? Luckily, there was a brave and generous soul in New Jersey. So we headed off road, pulling our convoy into the driveway, and descending, like refugees, with two weeks of laundry, two freaked-out dogs, and two women fearing for the Reho home front.

Our quartet spent the first day of our double date engaged in grocery store hand-to-hand combat. Too late for toilet paper, bottled water and "D" batteries, we stocked up on critical supplies like wine and chocolate pudding. Then, not homebound yet, we went to see *Rise of the Planet of the Apes*. I'd always wondered how the Tea Party got started.

Over the next three days we stayed glued to the gusting weathercasters. One hapless Jersey anchor reported a Code Gray situation. That seemed a bit, well, bland to us. What's a Tsunami, Code Beige? Dive! Dive! Dive! It's Code Taupe!

The reporters did a masterful job of reporting absolutely nothing new for three days running. Wind was coming, water was coming. Code Gray!!!

Frankly, I tried to avoid Code Yellow. I know how my dogs hate wind and rain, and feared they would befoul the carpets so I put them in Huggies. Moxie has such a biscuit belly that the Velcro tabs sprung and he looked like he was wearing a tutu. Imagine his humiliation.

On the Thursday and Friday night before the projected perfect storm, my family huddled at home in the RV on the driveway. But by Saturday morning, with ominous tornado warnings afoot, we fled to the brick and mortar house. Our first clue to the severity of the situation was that none of the piercing warning sirens coming from the TV offered the statement "This is not a test." Tornadoes were spotted all over Delaware, Jersey, and points north, and they would continue overnight Saturday.

Heeding advice, we ruled out second floor sleeping and pitched base camp in the windowless side of the living room. A sofa and loveseat would do for me and Bon, and we'd bring a blow-up mattress downstairs for our hostesses. Rise of the Planet of the Idiots. Laurel and Hardy should have deflated the inflatable first.

Upstairs, we wrestled the awkward queen size balloon onto its end, coming within millimeters of slicing it in half with the ceiling fan. Lunging to get it out of the way, we nearly put the mattress through the window. By this time we were gasping for air and crying from laugher, sure there'd be a flood, and not from the hurricane.

When we finally slid the amoeba down the staircase and situated it in our make-shift refugee camp it was time to hunker down and say Goodnight, Irene. That's when we learned that even if you mute the TV, the warning siren does not mute. Tornado be damned, we turned off the television.

Come dawn, a clown in the group woke us to strains of "There's Got to Be a Morning After." Very funny. All was quiet on the western front, as the storm had missed us entirely and headed for the unlikely target state of Vermont. The Poseidon was still in place on the driveway and we were all above water.

That's when the comedy show began. Those poor on-air bastards had been broadcasting live for days and now they were left to report that pretty much nothing at all had happened. News anchors stood in half an inch of water, hairdos askew, as gawkers stood off left on perfectly dry land. Talking heads begged people to send photos or video of any storm damage. We had reports of twigs down, lawn chairs overturned. Such was the dearth of reportable information.

But that was a good thing. That the hurricane missed us and Rehoboth was grand news. I am not one of the folks who complained about overkill regarding the evacuation, the dire warnings, and the calls for preparedness. It's great to know that city and town governments, all up and down the East Coast, were ready, locked and loaded, to provide bailouts, and this time it was the literal kind.

And ya know, if the BIG ONE, an earthquake, hurricane, or tornado had hit, those anti-government Tea Party Poopers would have been right there in line, waiting for the government to rescue them and provide services. Hypocrites heal thyselves.

So I hope it's bye bye hurricane season real soon. I'm glad Rehoboth was spared and sorry for the devastation in Vermont. But following the earthquake, hurricane, and tornado scare, I got home just in time for the ensuing pestilence of Labor Day traffic.

This is Fay J. reporting live from the beach. Code Tan.▼

October 2011
It Started with a Special Kind of Discount

As I sat at Womencrafts Bookstore in Provincetown during October Women's Week, signing books and chatting with the proprietors, I learned it was the 35th anniversary of the store. WOW. Time flies when you're having fun out of the closet.

Women poured into the shop to meet authors Georgia Beers, Marianne Martin, and Sally Bellerose—and I was honored to be sitting among them, signing books. As women went to the cash registers to pay for their books, we heard Karen, from her perch across the counter, totaling the purchases.

"Thanks, that will be $36," she told one woman, "but I'll give you the lesbian discount."

Lesbian discount. Instantly, it was more than 30 years ago and my first visit to Womencrafts.

I was an emotional train wreck that summer, newly divorced and perpetually confused. My former college roommate, straight as an arrow, invited me to spend a week in Hyannis on Cape Cod with her family. She knew I was happy to be out of the suffocating marriage but also knew I had no idea what to do next.

Always more perceptive and brave than I was, Lesley decided to take me to Provincetown for a day. We had lunch atop Pepe's, overlooking the bay, walked along Commercial Street and people watched. I saw sights that simultaneously intrigued and panicked me. I said not a word.

A happy-looking young woman pedaled by, her T-shirt proclaiming, "A woman without a man is like a fish without a bicycle." Really?

Then came a tall, muscular gal with a big button on her man-tailored shirt saying, "I'm the woman your mother warned you about." Shit. I was quieter still.

All ages, shapes and styles of women walked past, two by two, and many, hand in hand. We passed The Boatslip bar, where the boys were dancing to "Enough is Enough." Strains of "Hot Stuff" by Donna Summer and "Reunited" by Peaches & Herb filtered into the street.

When we got to Womencrafts, I went up the brick steps and inside while Lesley went down the steps to see about ear piercing. I poked around a bit in the shop, half-looking at, but not really absorbing the book titles. I decided to buy a ceramic tile with the image of Provincetown's Pilgrim Monument on it.

The friendly woman behind the counter wrapped up the tile, took my money and returned my change as she said, "And I gave you the lesbian discount."

Excuse me??? I could not get out of the store fast enough. Sweat welled on my forehead and my knees went to jelly. I practically ran down the steps to the street, where Lesley was already standing. I must have looked like a zombie.

"You okay?"

"Yeah."

"You don't look okay."

"Well," I said, guiding Lesley by the elbow into an adjacent alleyway. "In the store," I said, hushed, mumbling and pointing, "um...they gave me a...," getting quieter still, "lesbian discount," I whispered.

God bless Lesley for keeping a poker face and acting as if I'd said, "They gave me a ten percent discount."

She paused a minute, looked me in the eye and said, a hint of a smile forming, "You might want to think about that."

I stared at her, then past her, to a women with short, short hair and silver earrings all up and down her ears. Beyond her, two skinny men kissed on the street.

"You took me here on purpose, didn't you?"

"I did."

"Well, now you have to buy me a big drink on purpose."

Which she did. And as we sat at an outdoor café along the busy, funky, noisy street, with straight couples pushing baby strollers, outlandishly dressed drag queens, handsome gay men, and to my mind, even more handsome lesbians flooding by, we had the conversation that started to change my life.

To a subliminal soundtrack of Sister Sledge and "We are Fam-i-ly," we talked and talked. No, it was not the first time I'd thought about my attraction to women or wondered when I'd have the guts to do something about it. But it was the first time I'd said any of it out loud, either to myself or to another person.

Four hours later, as we left the tip of Cape Cod, with its artists, tea dances and lesbian discounts, for the very first time in years I knew exactly what direction I was going. And of course, since then, it's been quite a ride.

Lesley's gone now. The unspeakably cruel Huntington's Disease took her some years ago. But not before I'd settled down with Bonnie and we got to spend lots of cherished time and many adventures together. And I will always credit Lesley with the insight to give me that great big shove I needed.

I've had some amazing experiences in P-Town over the years, vacationing, visiting with friends, and since 2004, doing readings, book signings, and meeting and greeting readers and other writers. Women's Week there has a mini-literary festival component and I've been having a blast.

And Womencrafts is still there, alive at 35, still giving those wonderful lesbian discounts. I'm so lucky to have been the recipient of one in 1979, along with the gift of Lesley's friendship, setting me on my way toward my career as an activist and writer. Happy Birthday dear Womencrafts, happy birthday to you. ▼

November 2011

"You need to relax," my spouse warned after finding me pole vaulting over the furniture, screaming about politics, the price of gas and other indignities. "Maybe you need a massage."

Maybe, but I confess I'm intimidated by the world of massage therapists and their hot stones and new age music. Let's face it. Nobody's surprised I have trouble relaxing. Between my brain and my mouth going a mile a minute, I can't see myself as a candidate for massage, yoga, or any other calming pursuits. And I've tried. Lordy, I've tried.

Years ago we went so far as to install a double Jacuzzi tub at our house, hopeful for long, candle-lit baths, time spent sipping wine and winding down.

On our first plunge, we hopped in just as the hot water ran out, leaving us in 8 inches of tepid liquid. Our hot water heater was not up to the task. Eager to get to the candles and wine, we grabbed a spaghetti pot, filled it with water, set it boiling on the stove, then dumped the brew into the tub. There hasn't been so much running with pots of boiling water since Butterfly McQueen began birthing babies in *Gone With The Wind*. Not, relaxing.

So next, I tried yoga. My instructor is still laughing. I think she's laughing.

Skeptical and scared of displaying physical and mental inflexibility, I went to a Gentle Yoga class—which is a polite way of saying it's for the elasticity challenged. If I ever did manage to get my feet and wrists on the floor simultaneously, butt toward Mecca, the only thing to get me vertical again would be the winch on a tow truck. Or, they could just bronze me for a lawn ornament.

But I have to say, yoga is awfully non-judgmental. Nothing is a problem. If you can't stretch to a specific position, they give you a dowel in your hand to bridge the gap. Can't reach around your own thunder thighs to pull your knees to your chest? There's a canvas belt to help. I appreciated the assist, but I looked like a piece of furniture cinched into a Bekins Van. With all our innocent apparatus lying about, we also resembled S&M cultists.

You know, it is possible to relax too much. Under the heading of "that's okay, it's supposed to happen," certain yoga positions can cause flatulence. Everybody in our class, at one time or another, produced an audible emission. I don't think that praying you'll get through the hour without breaking wind is the kind of meditation we're encouraged to practice.

From yoga I moved on to mineral baths. My first experience was in New Mexico where it was 114 degrees. You could fry a frittata on the bench in front of the hotel. I got third degree burns of my frittata. But there was a famous mineral spring nearby we were counseled not to miss.

The rickety old bath house sat amid naturally swirling hot springs. I was led into a creaky closet-like room with a single claw foot tub. Now I know mineral water discolors everything in its path, but this old tub was so rusty and nasty I asked if the last tourist to bathe there had been Wyatt Earp. It was not relaxing.

Thinking a more modern roman bath might be the key, we traveled to the State Park Bathhouse at Berkley Springs, West Virginia. The newest fixtures in that place looked to be from the FDR Administration. That went for the staff, too.

After my soak in 750 gallons of mineral water, I was led to an antique massage table, where I was draped in a scratchy white sheet and rubbed down with a traditional mixture of olive oil and 190 proof ethyl alcohol. I felt like a wedge salad. And I was so slippery I began to slide off the table, saved only by the efforts of my 85-year old masseuse.

"When do you add the balsamic vinegar?" I asked. She was not amused and I was not relaxed.

A year later, still never having had what I considered to be a therapeutic massage, we went to China—home of the famous foot and full body massage. What the hell, I'd have to try it.

Our tour bus stopped at a building lit up like the Vegas strip, with flashing Chinese characters and marquee signs shouting Foot Massage! I didn't know if I was going for a medical procedure or a matinee of *Footloose*.

First they cooked my feet in herbal tea, then tossed me on a table and started thumping my shoulders, playing me like a bongo drum. Apparently my Qi energy was out of alignment, and that's bad. While a platoon of massagers pinched and pressed at acupressure points, I wondered if this was how the terra cotta warriors died. They called it Zone Therapy and this pudgy American was not in the zone. I couldn't wait to get back to the hotel and some Moo Goo Gai Pan.

Then, a year ago or so I had a sports injury (stop laughing). Due to my ridiculous golf swing I strained some cartilage in my sternum, so I saw a deep tissue massage therapist. While she cured my ailment, I can still feel the excruciating torture of her putting her elbow in my shoulder blade and trying to make it exit through my esophagus. Not relaxing, with a capital NOT.

So now I'm doing research. Just this afternoon I poured myself a martini and sat down to learn about all the different massage disciplines and what my next move should be. Do I want Swedish massage, Aromatherapy with essential oils or hot stone treatments? How about Shiatsu finger pressure or reflexology? You know, reading about this stuff, Schnauzers at my feet, with a drink in my hand, well, it's very, very, relaxing.

By George, I think I've got it. I've invented the Vodka with Essential Olives Therapy. Ask for the room with the Schnauzers. ▼

LEARNING TO CRAWL

I have now spent more money on one room in my house than on any other. And it's not even a room. It's the crawl space. Cue the scary music.

How I came to own a home with something called a crawl space is beyond me. What am I, from the Addams Family? Just the thought of the space and what could crawl in it makes me nuts. And I'm sure nobody is surprised I've never actually crawled into the crawl space to take a look at what's creeping around down there.

But that scary space beneath my home has, over the years, seen more inspections than Iraq's nuclear facilities.

Apparently, in the early 90s, building beach homes atop crawl spaces rather than concrete slabs seemed like a good idea. As with other fads gone bad, like Sir Walter Raleigh's idea to stick tobacco leaves in your mouth and set them on fire, to the more recent Fen-Phen diet craze, dangerous issues arose from the idea of crawl spaces. In our case we were told a river ran through it and toxic fungi festered down there.

The first crawl space incident happened several years ago. Mildew spots appeared on clothes in our guestroom closet. This was odd, as we no longer lived on a boat. My mate, always up for adventure, volunteered to belly crawl under the house to see what was breeding in the Petri dish under our spare room.

I watched House Detective disappear into the black hole, kneeled at the ground level entrance to the space and read aloud from the newspaper: " three bedroom, two bath CONDO…"

"Is there a fungus among us?" I hollered into the cavity.

"The moisture barrier seems okay," my spouse yelled. What? To me, a moisture barrier is a Totes umbrella.

"I don't see any black mold," came a faraway voice. Is that good? Does it relate to the stuff in Tupperware in my fridge?

Eventually my mate emerged, damp and mud-caked, admitting we needed professional help.

"It's not too bad. I've seen lots worse around here," said the contractor. Apparently, thanks to bad grading and too few vents, we had Lake Minnehaha under the house. No black mold, so cancel the bulldozer.

We could have bought a Kia for what it cost for a complex system of electronic vents and fans to blow out the moisture. Sometime later, convinced I'd developed acute Tinnitus or ringing in the ears, I went to the doctor, who assured me my ears were fine. I laughed when, days later, as I stood in my walk-in closet, ears ringing away, I realized I was hearing the incessant hum of my crawl space vents inhaling. I wanted my co-pay back.

But in no time, the crawl space was dry as a bone, even as the house occasionally sounded like LAX with jumbo jets taking off. Everything under the house was all well and good for a few years, until recently when Schnauzerhaven, a completely feline-free zone for obvious reasons, began to smell like a kitty litter box.

Clearly, a feral family had relocated to our crawl space. Once again, I sent my long-suffering mate, armed with a flashlight and Friskies, under the house. Nancy Drew discovered no cats. Just the overpowering aroma of Eau d' Kitty. Upstairs, the dogs went berserk, sniffing at the heating vents like teens huffing aerosols.

Coincidently, it was time for our quarterly exterminator visit (I live at the beach, ergo I have ants). As luck would have it, the bug hunter was getting into the lucrative field of crawl space remediation. Spiderman saw dollar signs.

He said there were no cats, but we had more than ants in our pants. We had under-house white water rapids and hazardous black mold. He recommended digging a maze of French drains and installing a giant sump pump. When his mold remediation credentials turned out to be a certificate for snuffing creepy-crawlers, I told Spiderman to take back the night and go home.

Then I called a company advertised as crawl space experts. Well, the second opinion was just as terrifying. They wanted to rent a giant dumpster, rip out all our under-house insulation, install miles of moisture barrier and dig up the circumference of our foundation.

I would have instantly posted a For Sale sign on the house, but realized that potential buyers would have to be willing to wear gas masks and bio hazard gear while watching TV. So I got the name of a highly recommended firm specializing in crawl space solutions.

These people not only emerged from under the house with good news, but with—here's a concept—good pictures. I could actually see what was happening in the forbidden zone and the answer was nothing much. No Lake Superior, no procreating mold, no Hello Kitty.

"You probably had some dampness under here with melting snow or after very heavy rains. And yeah, when insulation gets a little wet it smells just like cat pee." Aha! I knew my schnozz that could tell Merlot from Beaujolais couldn't mistake cat piss.

Okay, so we had a little mildew, a trickle of moisture now and then and our 14 year old moisture barrier was a shredded mess—probably from my spouse crawling on it every time I whiffed Sylvester and friends. Or, from Spiderman working in golf cleats.

We didn't need drains, sump pumps, or insulation ripped out. It was suggested that like 1950s ads with doctors endorsing Marlboros, our expensive crawl space vent system, sucking in air had seemed like a good idea at the time, but was no longer a remediation of choice.

"Actually, it's pumping cold air inside in the winter and hot air in the summer and boosting your heating bills." Ugh.

So our experts sealed up the vents, installed a silent dehumidifier and entombed the entire crawl space with a moisture barrier to keep water out, appropriate temperatures in and mold from forming. And when the insulation dried, the phantom cats left, too.

Photos of the finished job look amazing. The floor and four-foot walls are covered in clean, white vinyl material, the vents are gone, and a small, moisture-activated dehumidifier sits quietly off in a corner. It looks so lovely down there I'm considering setting up my laptop and a coffee pot and going into the cave to write.

But stay tuned for the next installment of Home Sweet Crawl Space, when some enterprising company figures out that crawl space encapsulation, like Asbestos before it, seemed like a good idea at the time. Cue the scary music...▼

January 2012

Thank goodness the cruise I took this winter was not the one that wound up on its side in Italy.

There's something to be said for being able to afford the Caribbean but not Europe. Watching that disaster unfold right after debarking from a cruise was very, very unsettling.

However, our own cruise was unsettled by the threat of the dreaded Norovirus or 24 hour flu, familiarly known as the trots. Picture this. We line up at the pier to board and nattily dressed cruise officials start squirting our palms with antibacterial gel. What is this, 1912 and I'm at Ellis Island being deloused?

We stand there, with thousands of other cruisers—a cornucopia of screaming babies, people coughing into their elbows, and suitcases having rolled through heavens knows what to be there—and wonder why, when picturing our dream vacation, this scene never came to mind?

Then we get the warning flyer. The previous ship had suffered an outbreak of Norovirus and over 400 people got sick. However, we're assured that the vessel has been thoroughly swabbed and disinfected and we are merely being cautioned by the Centers for Disease Control. I'm going on a cruise. I expect to be cautioned by Weight Watchers, not the CDC. The flyer warns me to wash my hands incessantly and take precautions against touching contaminated doorknobs and railings. What precautions? I'm going to Cozumel, I didn't bring mittens.

I flash back to my health conscious friends warning that effective hand washing requires 30 seconds in soapy water, which is roughly equivalent to the time it takes to sing the Birthday Song. Okay, I can do that.

As I board the ship I am again squirted with complimentary disinfectant. I'm surprised the gangplank photographer does not include the squirter patrol in each souvenir portrait. The ship is massive, like cruising in the mall. I need GPS to find my state-room.

After unpacking, I head upstairs to the lounge, touching the elevator button with the hem of my blouse. Going to the 12th floor, raises my shirt practically over my head. Which is worse, the trots or being a flasher? Looking down to avoid stares from the crowd I see that the elevator floor has a panel reading Saturday. They must change it daily. I'm facing six more days of epidemiological gymnastics?

From the lounge I visit the casino, where, to humor the CDC I keep a cocktail napkin around my Rum Punch glass. Then I stretch my shirtsleeve over my hand, pulling my neck and head to my shoulder, as I crank the one-armed bandit. Quasimodo at sea.

We go to dinner, getting squirted with the ubiquitous antibacterial gel on the way in and the way out. Thousands of people rub their hands together like mad villains planning nefarious deeds.

The next day, the unthinkable happens. I have to use a hallway rest room. Okay, primary mission accomplished, I go to wash my hands. I can do this..."Happy birthday to you, happy birthday to you, happy birthday dear Norovirus, happy birthday to you." Adjacent hand washers step away from the crazy lady.

It's a logistical cruelty that after banishing bacteria and blotting with a paper towel, you are forced to touch and turn the germ-riddled, outbreak-threatening, horror story of a door handle just to leave the bathroom. So I keep the soggy paper towel in my hand, open the door, hold it ajar with my ass and extend my too-short body toward the trash receptacle to dispose of my paper towel. A 7-foot NBA star couldn't sink it, if you'll excuse the word sink in a cruise article. Finally I give up, tuck the sodden towel in my pocket and exit.

Minutes later, lounging by the pool, contorting to hold a book while keeping my elbows and wrists off the infectious arms of the chair, I see that the wet paper towel has made a very unattractive wet spot on my shorts.

I get up to go change, heading for my room, when the boat hits an ocean swell, and I lurch forward, catching myself on the towel rental counter. Upright, but open-palmed, hands down on the shiny metal table, a thousand fingerprints look up and mock me.

The hell with it. I go get out of my wet shorts and into a dry martini.

And for the rest of the cruise I do not agonize about Norovirus. I augment the germicides by taking my alcohol internally and throwing precautions to the wind. I eat, drink and make merry. I dunk in the pool with the germy masses, sit amid coughing theatre crowds and touch any damn surface I please. I swim with dolphins, tour the islands, I'm king of the world.

Two days later, gleefully fingering the elevator buttons with my bare hands, I wonder if the removable day of the week panel might say, "It's Wednesday, do you know where your liver is?"

Then it's two more days of port visits, unrelenting gel squirts, more Bahama Mama cocktails for disease prevention and a grand time on the high seas. I knew it was time to come home when I looked down at my swollen ankles and realized I was retaining vodka. But thankfully, no signs of Norovirus.

I loved the cruise and didn't mind dripping with a little hand gel. But like other traumatic experiences, there can be flashbacks. As I watched the festivities after the Giants clinched the Super Bowl, I was absolutely horrified.

In a nightmare scenario, one dirty, sweaty, turf-covered player after another reached out with their bare hands to touch, and even oh-my-God kiss that darn Lombardi Trophy. Oh no, guys!!! Get thee to the soap dispenser and water supply. Sing Happy Birthday. Or you'll be in the bathroom when it's time to go to Disneyland.

As for me, I just bought stock in Lysol. Squirt, squirt.▼

DINNER FOR SEVEN

While an epidemic on the cruise ship was avoided, sometimes there is just no avoiding the homophobia bug. This particular cruise was a family vacation with my stepmom Joan, our son Eric, and his partner. So we grabbed a Royal Caribbean special, in lieu of our preferred Olivia cruise option and hoped for the best.

Me: "Hello, Royal Caribbean? Before I book this cruise, can I be totally certain our family can get a table for just the five of us in the dining room?"

RC: "Absolutely." I should have listened for the sound of their pants going up in flames.

On our first night aboard, New Years' Eve (after our lifeboat drill!), our gussied up party of five arrived at a table set for eight. As you can imagine, I immediately marched off to find the maitre 'd, who said he'd look into the snafu.

Returning tableside, I found two more travelers seated with us, a man and a woman. They were introducing themselves as recent retirees and newlyweds, from Iowa.

"That's wonderful," said Joan. "Congratulations to you. I'm here with my daughter and her partner who are celebrating their upcoming 30th anniversary!"

The newlyweds' faces went as white and starched as the tablecloth.

"And," said Joan, oblivious to their gape-jawed stares, "this is my grandson Eric and his partner."

The couple all but gagged. Happy New Year. What is it, 1956?

At which point, the appetizers arrived and the newlyweds clasped hands, bowed their heads and prayed—perhaps for culinary abundance but more probably for our souls. Either way, what ensued was a most uncomfortable meal, as we learned of the Iowans' upcoming Priest-accompanied pilgrimage to Rome so they could walk among the saints, countered by our attempt to discuss anything at all without mentioning our entire lives as sinners.

Finally, we gave up and got into the party favors, with Eric donning the Happy New Year tiara and me plunking the plastic top hat on my head. Eventually our contingent fled to the piano bar to await midnight.

Bright and early on day one of 2012, I was at the ship's customer service desk discussing dinner arrangements, sad that we still needed this discussion in 2012. The clerk stared blankly as I told of the embarrassing table introductions and our companions praying into their soup.

"Look," I said. "We're here for a relaxing vacation and this is beyond uncomfortable. I think these people were praying to save our souls. The only thing we need saving from is dinner with them."

"What?" said a passing supervisor. "Say what?"

I started repeating the story, and the very animated supervisor interrupted with, "Girl! You're kidding, they did what???"

I had found a friend of Dorothy (and if you don't know what that means, read on).

By dinnertime we had a private table for five, in a secluded alcove, with ultra-friendly wait staff and the start to a marvelous week of gourmet meals, Bahama Mama cocktails, celebratory toasts, and family bonding.

We'd also been directed to the bulletin board announcing a Friends of Dorothy cocktail party at 6 p.m. that night and every night of the cruise in an upstairs lounge. That evening we met several gay couples hailing from places like Chicago, Utah, Colorado, and even Singapore. We talked jobs, relationships and gay rights, and had a blast.

We did notice that the crowd seemed middle-aged and up. "I bet some of the younger folks don't even know the friends of Dorothy reference," somebody said, and I agreed.

So the next day, at the adult pool (thank goodness for that!) Bonnie and I spied some younger FOD candidates and mentioned the get-together. They were delighted, but had no idea that Friends of Dorothy was code for LGBT people.

"Dorothy, like in *The Wizard of Oz*? Like Judy Garland?" I ventured. They were clueless. Go figure. But they joined us that night, and throughout the week several more couples found us. It was just the addition to cruise activities we needed. And we loved introducing some of the more youthful homos to the secret codes of gay history.

As a whole, the cruise was delightful. The enormous ship had so many activities, bars, and restaurants, it didn't seem like there were 4,000 men, women and screaming children aboard. We made our own fun, including swimming with dolphins in Jamaica, touring beautiful Grand Cayman (but not spending money there, because we hate their homophobic politics) and soaking up sunshine, tequila and lime in Cozumel.

It did amuse us that the ship scheduled both a toga party and a 70s costume party onboard without advance word to travelers. I'd like to see them try that on a gay cruise. By happenstance, a surprising number of passengers had fashion-backward 70s wear in their regular wardrobes, so all was saved. We traded seeing middle America in togas and bell-bottoms for the ice-dancing show (lots of friends of Dorothy on the ice) and the Royal Caribbean Broadway Review (more boys from Oz).

When we weren't going metaphorically overboard eating or drinking, we spent the remaining fraction of time at the pool, piano bar, spa, or in our cabin. Joan, Bonnie, and I shared a stateroom and Bonnie was assigned the upper bunk. She won the honor because she, unlike Joan or myself, did not require a 3 a.m. potty break. I know, TMI. But I didn't want you to think it was random cruelty toward my spouse.

Actually, sharing the cabin worked well, and it should be noted that the most chronologically mature traveler among us was the one who wanted to stay up the latest and party the most. Go Joan!

A straight cruise is fine for a visit, but I wouldn't want to live there. My friend Dorothy would click her ruby red slippers, take us back to Gayberry and exclaim, "There's no place like home."▼

February 2012

As a college freshman, in 1966, I went to see the Broadway musical *Mame* with my high school sweetheart. He was an adorable musical comedy devotee on the verge of leaping out of the closet. I was still more than a dozen years away from coming out and becoming a lesbian anachronism—a female musical comedy queen.

We adored *Mame* for its humor, style, and most of all, heart. And we loved its star, Angela Lansbury, then in her early 40s, for pretty much the same reasons. We treasured her and Bea Arthur, later TV's Maude, singing the friendship anthem "Bosom Buddies."

I was so taken with the show and its star I followed up by watching every old movie—*The Harvey Girls*, *Gas Light*, *Manchurian Candidate*—Lansbury ever filmed.

Then, holiday season 1968, when my mother was working for the Actor's Fund of America, I volunteered to be a theater "basket passer," collecting money at intermission for the Actor's Fund Home in New Jersey. Basket passers got free tickets. In prior years, home for college vacation, I would see eight shows in a holiday week. In 1968, however, I practically camped at the Winter Garden Theatre, passing the basket at eight consecutive performances of *Mame*. I met the cast between the matinee and evening shows and mingled backstage. I was a *Mame* groupie before that term was coined. Angela Lansbury was gracious and warm to this star struck teenage hanger-on.

When my mother died from breast cancer the next year, at age 49, it was a shocking and horrible blow. But I didn't meet it head on. I swallowed my grief, put off dealing with it, and threw myself into my own blossoming theater career. I gobbled up as much live theater and theater lore as I could. That included seeing Angela Lansbury again in the short-lived musical *Dear World*. It was a showcase for her, but not as the glamorous star everyone wanted to see after *Mame*. Still, I loved hanging over the back wall in standing room, watching her work.

Grief. Denied. Sexuality. Denied. Life. Making do. Theater kept me grounded while I flailed around socially, finally marrying a man to prove my normalcy. I fed my emotions with musical comedy humor and happy endings, and made do with intense friendships with the leading ladies I was directing.

In 1971, I was lucky enough to get a balcony ticket to the Tony Awards 25th Anniversary Celebration, where I saw Angela and Bea Arthur in a sparkling recreation of "Bosom Buddies." Then in 73 Angela came to Washington, DC, in *Gypsy* at the Kennedy Center. I worshipped at the altar at least twice, maybe three times. A year later Angela appeared with a tour of *Mame* at a tent theater and again, I was there, soaking up the glow.

When, in 1978, I finally got my chance to direct my own production of *Mame*, my make-do marriage was crumbling and my whole world was held together by my theatrical adventures. I wrote a fan letter to Ms. Lansbury that summer, telling her about my production and letting her know that my director's note for the program would dedicate the show to her. I felt silly the moment I put the note in the mailbox.

One week later, just before opening night, I received a hand-written letter in blue ink on light blue Tiffany stationery from Mame herself, wishing me and the cast well. She noted her delight at having the show dedicated to her performance of a dozen years before.

Over the next few years, as I contemplated poking my head out of the closet, I continued directing and listening to *Mame*, *Gypsy*, and other Lansbury recordings until the vinyl wore out. I was in New York for a 1979 preview performance of Angela's Tony Award-winning performance in *Sweeny Todd*. They hadn't quite worked out the special effects yet, and sitting in the second row, I was happily splashed with fake blood from the grisly musical. I loved it and listened to the cassette tape of the music all the way home.

Then, in 1980 my life righted itself. I finally leapt from my self-imposed, self-hating closet and dealt with much of my emotional baggage. After some early escapades and laughable misadventures dating women, I finally met a great group of friends. Two years later I met Bonnie.

"Who's Angela Lansbury?" she asked. It was opposites attracting. She'd seen a touring musical or two but was by no means the theatre nut I was. For my part, I got to learn about softball.

In July 1983, on our way home from a week in Provincetown, I snagged tickets for a just-opened revival of *Mame*, with Angela re-creating her role. This was just before she became a household name in TV's *Murder, She Wrote*. Maybe Ms. Lansbury had insufficient star power for a new generation, or maybe rock musicals were eclipsing the golden age classics, but, after glowing reviews but disappointing box office numbers, the show had already posted its closing notice.

But it didn't disappoint me. Bonnie and I cheered for the joyous and faithful revival, starring my favorite performer. I wondered if the producers remounted the show just so Bonnie and I could share an experience that had meant so much to me.

As Bonnie and I built a life together, Angela Lansbury solved scripted murders. She spent the next dozen years as sleuth Jessica Fletcher, winning Emmy Awards and entertaining millions. Only after the series ended, and she took a good long time off, did she make her way back to Broadway.

It was the new millennium by then and we were all getting older. If Bonnie and I were headed for our 60s, Angela was entering her 80s. When it was announced she'd return to Broadway in the two-woman show *Deuce*, about aging tennis rivals, we knew we had to be there. After all, how many more times would she appear on the Great White Way?

Plenty, as it turns out. *Deuce* was an anemic vehicle, panned by critics who raved about Angela anyway. It was bliss watching her verbally decimate the show's second character, as she used some quite un-Lansbury language. Shockingly fun.

Her next vehicle was the comedy *Blithe Spirit* and again we ran to Broadway. "After all, she's at least 83 by now. This could be her last show." Ha! Next came the role of the Countess in Sondheim's *A Little Night Music*. Bonnie and I started to joke about going broke on her farewell performances.

Then, back in December 2010 came the piece de resistance. A friend asked me to volunteer backstage at the Kennedy Center Honors in Washington, DC. Songwriter-lyricist Jerry Herman, who wrote *Mame, Hello Dolly!*, and *La Cage Aux Folles* was an honoree. Nobody knew yet who'd be on tap to give tribute and perform for Jerry, but we had mighty high hopes.

It was still hush-hush the week before the event when a clue came from a member of the Gay Men's Chorus of Washington. The group was invited to perform "The Best of Times is Now" from *La Cage*. Penciled onto their sheet music for the verse were the names Chita, Carol and Angela. Chita Rivera? Carol Channing? Angela? I was a wreck with excitement.

My friends and I were assigned as escorts to the stars set to appear in the tribute to Jerry. Other cast members included Christine Baranski, Christine Ebersole, Matthew Morrison from Glee, and many more. Other tributes were going out to Sir Paul McCartney and Oprah, so this was not going to be a light-weight evening backstage. But for me, being in the wings with Angela Lansbury would be a fantasy come to life.

Volunteer rules were strict: no photos, no special requests, just do your job and be professional. On the rehearsal day before the Honors show, I arrived at Kennedy Center early to escort a college chorus from Oprah's Alma Mater to their rehearsal. When my job was done I walked down the hall to one of the rehearsal rooms. As I approached, my friend Patrick appeared, with none other than Carol Channing on his arm. Frail at nearly 90, her wigged head and artfully made up countenance still presented a confident, bigger than life Dolly Levi.

"Miss Channing, this is my friend Fay."

And in that inimitable voice, with its liquid vowels, Miss Channing said, "Hell-yow, Fay," as if she'd uttered 'Hell-yow, Dolly," and I thought I'd melt to the floor.

I followed Patrick and Carol into the rehearsal room, where I stopped and stared. At the piano stood Angela, tall and elegant in a brown tweed blazer and perfectly pressed trousers. Chita Rivera stood beside her in a stunning black turban and a flowing black outfit. Miss Channing slowly made her way to them.

Next, came one of the kindest, most generous moments I've ever witnessed, as superstars Chita and Angela helped the slightly befuddled Channing with the words and simple choreography for their musical number. With a Broadway legend on each arm, Carol Channing, at least a legend and a half, came alive—and the trio brought down the room. No doubt, bringing down the house would come later.

A lot of wondrous things happened that day and the next. As I was introduced to Angela Lansbury by her escort, I tried not to be a blubbering fool. She looked so energetic and youthful for 84, with her ramrod posture, and quiet, graceful demeanor. I wound up having a short conversation with her during a break, mentioning my Actor's Fund experience at *Mame*. Angela was gracious and sweet to me, then smiling broadly but with melancholy, she spoke of her bosom buddy Bea Arthur who had recently passed away.

By Sunday morning, the day of the show, the pace quickened. At dress rehearsal all afternoon, I found myself milling about backstage with the casts of all the tributes, plus the elegant Caroline Kennedy, the lovely Jennifer Hudson, and the surprisingly grumpy Chris Rock.

As the curtain rose that night, Angela, dressed in a shimmering silver outfit, began the Jerry Herman tribute standing at a lectern, summarizing his musical career. When a five minute video came on, the stage lights dimmed and Angela walked backstage left and stood right next to me. When the film highlighted Jerry's ambitious flop *Dear World*, Angela shook her head, looked at me and said, "They just didn't want to see Auntie Mame look so frumpy."

Instantly, I was that 20 year-old, with my standing room ticket, watching *Dear World* and thinking the exact same thing.

As I stood in Angela's shadow in the wings, we watched Carol Channing open the musical part of the tribute with, what else, "Well, well, Hello, Jerry…" followed by singers and dancers celebrating his best words and music. Chita Rivera swept onto the stage from the opposite side, singing a song from *Dear World*. On the first notes, she gazed directly, with great affection, at Angela in the wings before turning her head to the crowd.

Minutes later, Christine Ebersole and Christine Baranski took the stage to sing "Bosom Buddies." The instant the intro began, Angela smiled and began moving to the music. So did I. She glanced at me to her right, winked and started mouthing the words, adding some in-place choreography. And for about a minute and a half, the two of us stood together, miming the number and smiling like fools.

I've struggled to find the perfect words to describe how I felt during those 90 seconds, but I can only come close. Thrilled, of course; bursting with emotion, sure; a life cycle of emotion spanning more than 40 years from my scared and conflicted youth, to my secure, satisfying present. Absolutely.

For the tribute finale, it was left to Angela, Chita and Carol, backed by the Gay Men's Chorus to sing Jerry's words that probably do sum it up for me. "The best of times is now." And Angela Lansbury has been with me for almost the whole ride.

I never did volunteer again for Kennedy Center. I just didn't want to clutter up the memory of that night. Long may my idol wave, long may I rave. To my mind, we've always been bosom buddies. ▼

February 2012

It's an amazing insight when you realize you've been eating, drinking and suffering along with the Oscar telecast with the same people for almost 40 years. At first revelation you think, "How is this even possible?" Then you go to "Damn, we're old," and finally you settle into "Isn't this absolutely wonderful."

So it was on the afternoon of Feb. 26 when I realized I've been "doing the Oscars" since the mid-1970s with my pals Don and Lee. In a stunning example of "The more things change the more they stay the same," our lives, hometowns and even my sexual orientation changed (okay, revealed itself!) in the interim, but we are still sitting through the Sunday night telecast drinking, laughing and making snarky comments.

Frankly, the tenor and quality of the comments has remained biting and hilarious (at least to us), even though the term snarky wasn't even invented when we started bitching and moaning about the jokes and fashion faux pas. But, as it is now defined—**snark•i•ly**\adverb, *Rudely sarcastic or disrespectful; snide*—we believe our prior performances were plenty snarcastic.

Our run began in 1974 when Nixon left and *Cuckoo's Nest* was Best Picture. Coincidence? That was followed by host Bob Hope (with Farrah Fawcett's gorgeousness leaving a snark free zone), then Johnny Carson hosted through 1981. For reference, that was the year that Paul McCartney and Stevie Wonder did "Ebony and Ivory." When Bonnie joined Don, Lee and me in 1983 (I missed current events that year, as I was besotted with young love!), and our new quartet watched Meryl win her first for *Sophie's Choice*.

We forged ahead in my 40th year, with Cher's strategically placed sequins to discuss in '88 as she won for *Moonstruck*, then '89 with Demi Moore in a bustier and biker shorts. What was she thinking? When was it that Cher wore her black winged feathered dress? By the mid 90s we were starting to weekend in Rehoboth and sometimes the Oscar parties, hosted on TV by Billy Crystal, were here in our weekend places. Such was '95 with *Forrest Gump*, as host Whoopi tried to curb her raging snark and stay out of trouble. She did not.

It was in 2000, Bonnie and I were Rehoboth full-timers by then, when Angelina showed up all Goth with her blood vial. The next year singer Björk wore that ridiculous swan dress with the dead bird around her neck and the outfit was parodied so brilliantly by Ellen DeGeneres, at her Emmy host job right after. I'm sure we were off the scale on the snarkometer that night.

And so it went, as Don and Lee moved to the beach full-time as well, and we watched a parade of Oscar hosts, more Billy Crystal, some gorgeous superstars—notably Hilary Swank, Julia Roberts, and Halle Berry looking hot, with George Clooney, Ralph Fiennes, and Colin Firth captivating the boys.

Through the years our food and beverage choices changed—unrepentant carbs and comfort food when we were puppies, healthier eating in the mid-years, and now back to comfort food again, but with guilt.

Every year since the beginning we've had ballots and quizzes compliments of Don, and every year we agonize over the same question: Do we select who we think will win, or who we want to win? For years we had prizes, too, but that seems to have stopped since we are all trying to winnow down our clutter.

So here we were again in 2012. Somebody said, "Nothing like a red carpet show to remind us that actors need writers." And we were glad we weren't hosting since Billy Crystal was looking very, very puffy.

"Don't look in the bathroom mirror," somebody added.

Then, iPad addicts that we'd become, we discovered we could augment our own snarkiness by logging on to Snark Food, a website for "freeing your inner snark." Several people posted comments like "Handlers should run with these movie stars like at the *Westminster Dog Show*," and "Billy may be late tonight, he's coming all the way from the 80s." My favorite was "Billy Crystal has had so much work done he's looking like Kim Jong Il."

Funny, but nobody dared look in the mirror. ▼

THE BEST OF TIMES IS NOW

The wedding wasn't supposed to be that big a deal—just a smattering of family and out of town friends to join us for the Jewish wedding we never got to have. What could be so difficult? Now that Delaware had a civil union law, we'd make our 2003 Canadian wedding official here at home.

The escalation began when the rabbi and her soon-to-be-wife sat sipping wine with us, asking a few questions.

"Are you going to have a Ketubah?"

Bonnie, a Jew for a couple of minutes now, knew exactly what that was. Me, a Jew from birth, not so much. A Ketubah is a marriage contract, kind of a pre-nup, without talk of finances, with beautiful artwork and prose, to be signed by the couple, witnesses, and officiant.

"Great, where do I get one, Ketubahs R Us?"

I wasn't far off. Ketubahs.com had zillions of pretty pictures, with gooey wording at equally gooey prices. They offered overnight shipping. What? For shotgun weddings?

There actually were two choices of wording for same-sex couples, but neither prose recognized the 30 years Bonnie and I have already been together, which we wanted to note. So, going rogue, we wrote our own words, and had graphic genius Murray Archibald superimpose the copy on a pretty picture we'd taken. Voila! Ketubahs really are us.

Of course, we wanted to have the ceremony at the community room at CAMP Rehoboth, figuring a few hors d'oeuvres, a little bubbly, and music by iPod. Brides plan, friends and wedding planners laugh.

Within a few weeks of the ceremony I had hired a piano player and gotten into a discussion with my step-mom Joan about the kind of flowers we were having.

Joan: "What kind of flowers are you having?"

Me: "Flowers?"

So I called my pal Chris Beagle, the wedding planner, for advice. He discussed so many options my head exploded.

Me: "Okay, Uncle! Will you be my wedding planner and do the flowers?"

Chris: "Sure. We'll need two large arrangements and one at the table with the guest book."

Me: "Guest Book???"

So I found myself at Michael's Crafts in the Wedding aisle, alongside several size four teenage brides-to-be picking out guest books. They all assumed I was the mother of a bride, or omigod, grandmother of a bride. I haven't felt so out of place since I accidentally wandered onto a softball field.

Chris: "I know Mixx is catering, but who's handling the table cloths?"

Me: "Table cloths?"

That's when I turned it all over to Chris—caterer liaison, flower arrangement, and even the construction of the wedding canopy or Chuppah—you can pronounce it properly by clearing your throat on the "Ch."

By the day before the wedding, the rabbi reminded me we needed a glass for Bonnie to stomp at the end of the ceremony. I wandered around Pier One, feeling up the glassware to find the most delicate glass to smash. We didn't want Bonnie stomping the thing with her dress shoe and honeymooning at the ER with shards in her instep. I found a perfect cheap champagne flute. The clerk must see this a lot, because he didn't look at me like I had two heads for buying a single glass.

That afternoon I got a phone call from an old friend, about to address our wedding card.

Friend: "After the wedding will you two be hyphenates?"

Me: "No, I think we will still be homosexuals."

By Monday evening, 24 hours and counting, Bonnie was calm but I was nervous. Not about the marriage. After thirty years, the only nerve-wracking part would be trying to remember our wedding anniversary. Which is why the event was on a Tuesday. Long ago we had deemed March 27 as our anniversary date and this year, our 30th anniversary, it would also be our big fat Jewish wedding. We are too old to memorize a new date. I was just nervous about logistics. I wanted to get hitched without a hitch.

My sister Gwen: "Are one of you staying at a hotel tonight? You aren't supposed to see the bride before the wedding."

Me: "Puleeeze."

On Tuesday morning, my wedding planner called.

Chris: "Do you need anything?"

Me: "Xanax."

And so it went. Cool cucumber Bonnie even went to work for part of the day, while Bridezilla here anxiously entertained visiting family and friends.

Then, at 5 p.m., after Bonnie and I dressed, we made sure we had the rings in our pockets and the delicate wine glass wrapped in a cloth napkin. That's so we wouldn't have to spend months picking glass shards out of the CAMP carpet.

Zero hour. Bonnie calmly announced she'd get the car from the garage and meet us on the driveway. Exiting the garage she backed right into the side of my stepmom's car. Not nervous?

She ran to the front door, horrified, wondering if she should be the runaway bride. Then we made our first vow of the day, agreeing to keep the incident secret until later. To that end, it was like a sitcom as we hustled Joan and Gwen into the car, shielding their view of Joan's dinged bumper. Get me to the church on time!

The room at CAMP looked gorgeous. Chris got his inner gay boy on, having built the most amazing canopy and making the room look country club elegant and not the least bit Vegas wedding chapel tacky.

The crowd was joyous, happy for us and happy that such a ceremony was legal in Delaware. Bonnie and I felt blessed to be in the company of family and longtime friends who traveled to Rehoboth from the likes of New York, Virginia, DC, and even Nova Scotia, despite it being a Tuesday.

And Rabbi Beth did an incredible job. She invited friends to provide blessings and allowed us to sip Châteauneuf-du-Pape wine instead of Manischewitz since to my mind, nobody should start their next 30 years with wine that tastes like Robitussin. The rabbi quoted from the Bible as well as songwriter Jerry Herman, with his lyrics "The Best of Times is Now."

Yes it is. Mazel Tov to all the couples who have come before us and all those to follow.

And for the record, Joan's car wasn't badly damaged. We joked that ours was the first Jewish wedding where we smashed a glass and a Prius. ▼

Temperanceville? Really? Have you met me?

When RV-owning friends asked us to caravan for a weekend in Temperanceville, VA, the very name Temperanceville gave me the yips. Had the historic town, associated with the Women's Christian Temperance Union, ever lifted its prohibition policy?

Hey, I'm a fair weather camper. Take away my Cosmopolitan and it's just rehab with mosquitoes. I called the campground asking if evil liquor would be allowed to touch our lips there. From sounds in the background, not only was it allowed, it appeared to be encouraged.

Armed with a fully stocked bar and eschewing teetotalism, we set out along the Delaware coast, heading for the Mason-Dixon line. First stop in Virginia was Dixieland Gas. If the South rises again, it will be here. I've never seen so many Confederate souvenirs in my life, and tempting as it was, I opted against the Picket's Charge tote-bag and went back outside.

There, the RV was as dead as Robert E. Lee. My mate sought jumper cables as I encountered a woman admiring our rig.

She: "I've always wanted an RV but could never afford one."

Me: "You can have this one."

We got a jump but needed not one new battery, but two. Apparently, lightning had struck one night recently and destroyed the under-rig battery, which, in turn, drained the one under the hood. I guess we lucked out the strike didn't burn down the RV and the house with it. Or did we?

Me: "Do we have replacement value insurance?"

Mate: "Yup."

Me: "Wow, that could have funded lots of five star hotels."

When the nasty stare ebbed I learned something. An errant battery part had melted, requiring my spouse to use the fire-starter gun to heat and shrink wrap the rubber battery cable cover like a lamb chop for the freezer. As we stood, toasting the battery compartment, my fears about detonating our second largest asset were not calmed by the sight, next door, of the Miracle Tabernacle Church and Pawn Shop.

Eventually we hit Temperanceville, where the beautiful campground faced Pocomoke Sound, and we situated our traveling condos to make a private courtyard for folding tables and chairs, Schnauzer dog beds, and iPod speakers. I love camping.

Building a fire is outside my skill set so I fiddled while my companions tried to get Rome to burn. Across the way, a camouflage-wearing, beer-bellied Yeti look-alike pulled out a propane torch and whoooosh, instantly lit his campfire. Also his eyebrows. Look away! Look away! Look away! Dixie Land.

Those folks were all finished barbecuing supper and themselves by the time our fire started to crackle. Fortunately, we'd already cooked our Kosher hot dogs on the electric griddle and beans in the electric crock pot. I love camping.

It does say something about our fluid commitment to renewable energy and recycling that we scrupulously separated all our beer bottles, but used disposable plastic liners in the crock pot. Well, it did save our personal energy.

There was an amazing full moon, as we sat around the fire, martinis in hand, anti-saloon league drop-outs telling stories of childhoods spent on the farm eating rhubarb pie, shucking fresh-picked corn and wringing the necks of chickens. Well, the other three did. Best I could offer was ordering chicken broth with matzo balls and wanting to wring the neck of the waiter who put his thumb in the soup.

Camper friend: "What kind of music is this?"

Me: "*Hello, Dolly!*."

Camper Friend: "I don't believe this."

Me: "I love camping."

We also discussed our comprehensive RV departure lists, always meticulously checked before heading out on a trip. Extra fuses, check; emergency food and drink, check; unhooking the rig from garage electric so we don't drag the three-bedroom rancher with us, check.

At which point my cell phone rang (if a cell phone rings in the forest and there's no one to hear it, are there still overage charges?). It was my neighbor telling me we'd left our garage door wide open. So much for checklists.

The night was still young but we were not, so pretty soon bed beckoned. Besides, there's only so much fresh air with a hint of Deep Woods Off I can take. The next thing I know it's dawn and my spouse comes back from a dog walk covered head to toe in thick brown mud, a veritable human sludgesicle.

Seems that a squatting Schnauzer had the acrobatic fortitude to poop on the steep side of a hill by a drainage ditch. A conscientious citizen, my mate bent to retrieve the specimen, lost her footing and, like a car crash dummy in a Kia, suffered a roll-over into the ditch. And apparently, climbing back out required gymnastics, if not crampons and ropes. We saw forensic evidence of the struggle when we went to view the scene of the slime.

Camper friend: "Wow, it looks like a college football game was played in there."

Camper friend 2: "I can see body parts sculpted into the muck."

Me: "Yeah, fossilized forms like at the La Brea tar pits..."

We hosed off the accident victim (memo to self: add extra shoes and pants to checklist), spent a day at Chincoteague visiting the beautiful beach and wild ponies, had a fried seafood lunch along the ocean, then stopped for dessert. One of the homemade ice-cream choices was actually Chocolate Marsh Mud. We deferred to Rocky Road.

Then came a second glorious evening around the crackling campfire, chowing down on microwaved linguini and clam sauce, sipping white wine. I do not believe there is a

Girl Scout badge offered for the making of this meal.

After dining, we offered dueling tales (thankfully, not dueling banjos) of farm animals and Broadway legends, along with copious anti-temperance league activities. And while the league may have succeeded in enacting Prohibition in the early 20th century, the term temperance originated to mean moderation in the indulgence of all the appetites. I know it was aimed at the first degenerates to sit around a camp fire making chocolate and marshmallow S'Mores.

Back at home, after a weekend of intemperate eating and drinking, it was tough to face the bathroom scale. Look away! Look away! Look away! Dixie Land. ▼

OUT! OUT! DAMNED...

They say that good fences make good neighbors. Not on my street. We love our neighbors. Although in this case, a big bottle of Febreze might make better neighbors.

One day recently I saw several cars on my neighbors' driveway, figured they were in town and walked across the street to find them. There, in the garage, stood Neighbor One and a pal, each holding a black and white furry baby in their arms. The women wore sly smiles.

"Want a kitten?" asked Neighbor One.

I eyed the long bushy tails on the fur babies suspiciously. "What are they, baby skunks?" I asked, warily.

"Yes," said the pal, who was volunteering for some kind of wildlife rehab organization. "Aren't they cute?"

"Yes, but aren't they going to spray you? How can you just hold them like that?"

"Oh, they're too young to spray yet," said the volunteer. "We've been holding them for a half hour and they're fine. Want to hold one?"

I held out my hands, and cradled one of the pointy-nosed, bright-eyed cuties in my arms. The little bastard looked up at me, and, apparently struck by sudden puberty, let loose with some sort of aerosol from his butt and EWWWWWW.

I tossed junior back to the volunteer, just as the girls started wrinkling their noses and backing away from me. Step away from the Fay.

I've been skunked before, by a contractor who failed to finish a job, or, my sister who usually sticks me with the check, but this was getting skunked in the stinkily literal sense.

PEE-EW. I stood there, reeking. "Why me?" I looked at the two women still holding black and white fur balls. You've been cuddling these skunklets for a half hour and nothing. He takes one look at me and hurls a stink bomb. So much for them being too young to vote. Shit."

"It's not so bad," said the volunteer, "it will go away in a minute. He's just a baby." I bent down and wiped my hands on a towel on the garage floor and then sniffed my palms. AUUGGGHHH!!!!

At which point Neighbor Number Two entered the garage saying, "Omigod. I'd know that smell anywhere!" Getting the gist of what happened, she said, "You have to get those clothes off, and not over your head or your hair will stink. And don't even put them in the trash, you have to find a dumpster, or burn them, omigod."

And with that, she grabbed a scissors, saying, "I'm going to help you," and cut my new golf shirt down the back and started to peel it off me.

"Wait, I have to get across the street first," I hollered, understanding that our road is a busy cut-through for traffic and not wanting to be in the newspaper as the Seaside Drive Lady Godiva. That could have caused a pile up or two.

So I started hauling butt across the street, my shirt flapping open in the back like a hospital gown. Neighbor Two caught up with me, walking behind me to keep me decent. When I hit my driveway, she retreated, I opened the garage door, closed it (this is important) and stripped. It's a very odd feeling standing buck naked in your own garage, stuffing your clothes in a plastic bag and sealing the bag like it contains Anthrax.

So I went inside, showered twice, lathered, rinsed and repeated ad nauseam, and finally emerged in clean clothes. Most of me was okay, but my right palm still had an eau d'skunklet aroma.

Recalling the old wives' advice to wash in tomato juice when you are skunk sprayed, I grabbed a bottle from the cabinet, put some ice, vodka and the tomato juice in a glass and had a few sips. Then, I stood over the sink and poured the remaining tomato juice over my hands. Handwringing ensued. Perhaps over how many Bloody Marys died in this process.

During the next several hours I crossed my palm with Febreze, Glade solid, Ban deodorant, and a variety of hand creams. Honestly, there is just a hint of skunk aroma left. I imagine it will dissipate before we next have to shake hands.

I suspect that "They're too young to spray" now belongs in the hall of fame with "You can't get pregnant the first time," and "The check's in the mail."

When Bonnie came home and heard the story, she banished me to the porch until she was sure there was an all-clear. Out there, I paced like Lady Macbeth, rubbing my hands together, channeling some crazed Shakespearian, staring at my palm and yelling, "Out! Out! Damned Skunk." Just to be safe, I had another Bloody Mary for internal protection and soaked my palm in some more tomato juice. Perhaps Clamato would have been better. Darn, I could have had a V8.

When Bonnie and Moxie agreed that I passed the sniff test, I was allowed back in the house. In the ensuing days I discovered that half the lesbians in Rehoboth had been playing with those skunk babies, and nobody but me got spritzed. Lucky me.

No harm, no foul, except for the loss of a great golf shirt, a ridiculously expensive brassiere, and my pride. It's tough knowing you're the only one who got skunked. But hell, I choose to think of it as a gift from that stinky little fellow. He made this *Letters* deadline a no brainer.

Thanks, little buddy. Sing with me. "Arrivederci, aroma."▼

April 2012

My house is now a Schnauzer geriatric ward. Like us, my boys are aging fast, but since dog years fly by faster than human ones, our house is in the full throes of canine old age. Paddy is 13 and Moxie is 14. I can hardly believe it. It seems like only yesterday they were teething on the furniture. These days, they're gumming.

Moxie's deaf and Paddy's blind, so between them they're one guard dog. Both boys still eat like animals, can sniff a Thrasher's french fry at 90 yards, and enjoy a moderate amount of exercise. When they wake up and discover strangers in the house they still go into their vicious guard dog routine despite the fact our guests have been in the building for hours.

It's also possible a little doggie dementia is going on, so they just as often bark hysterically in the middle of the night when absolutely nothing is happening. For a while we'd leap up, on full alert, ready to call 911, but now we just humor them, roll over, and try to sleep. Sometimes I think it's merely Paddy hearing Moxie snore. That dog needs a sleep study and a breathing device.

And if a doorbell goes off on television, Paddy jumps straight up into the air, alerting Moxie with his movement and both of them knock themselves senseless with the furniture they're under.

The Golden Years really began when Paddy couldn't walk by the water bowl without filling up or get through the night without emptying out. He's a full-on diabetic now, requiring us to administer two daily insulin injections.

There's a reason I'm a writer and not a health care provider. Squeamish-r-us. Based on our abilities, I'd say that Bonnie is the one who gives the skilled care around here. I'm more like the janitor.

But given our crazy schedules, both doggie parents had to

learn to give the injections. Bonnie was a natural. As for me, I'd close my eyes, steel myself, and stab the dog, who wouldn't even notice. But, I really should get my own eyes checked, because more often than not, when putting the cap back on the needle I stab myself in the thumb and shriek in a decibel level even Moxie can hear.

One day, the phone rang as I prepared to inject the insulin and behind my back the dogs switched food bowls. Believe me, when I gave Moxie the booster shot in the butt he was one surprised little Schnauzer. I panicked, calling the vet, hollering about giving insulin to the wrong patient.

"Don't worry," said the doctor, "just give Moxie a little sugar." I gave him a marshmallow Peep and he's been a Peepoholic ever since.

And what do we do with all those used needles? You can't just throw them in the trash. Between trips to the animal hospital to turn them in, we keep them in a big plastic pretzel jar. It looks like a candy dish for the Addams Family.

Setting a dog's insulin level is harder than for a human. And, until we found the right dose, Paddy gave us quite a winter. At its worst, he was up every two hours to pee. For a while, Bonnie and I took turns getting up and neither of us had a decent night's rest. Then we alternated for a whole night, making me a zombie only every other day. And it's a good thing it was a mild winter. We spent most nights in the yard in our pajamas.

Finally, we tried cutting a tail hole in Depends and it worked pretty well. Vanity is me, I cannot go through the Food Lion checkout without saying, "They're for my dog."

As for Moxie, at first I accused him of being passive aggressive. He wouldn't come when called but would respond instantly if I opened a bag of Utz potato chips. As an aside, Bonnie believes this about me, too, and she may be right. But for Moxie, I learned that voice pitch is the first to go, so I have cut him a break on responding to commands. If I need him in a hurry I'll rip open Doritos. Sometimes he hears me if I talk in a basso profundo like Tallulah Bankhead.

Also, just like their human counterparts, if the dogs could talk, they'd sit around discussing their ailments. I can just imagine Moxie complaining about his hearing deficit, and saying, "Come again?" when Paddy asks him to be his seeing-eye dog. They are co-dependent in a good way.

It was clear the twilight years were upon us when, last week, a bird flew into our sun room and neither dog noticed it. Up to that point it was Schnauzers 4, birds 0. Likewise, no bunnies were harmed in the making of this spring in Rehoboth.

Here at Schnauzerhaven Assisted Living, of course we offer free transportation within the area to doctors' appointments and the local beauty salon. We provide assistance with bathing and dressing ("Does this collar make me look fat?"), plenty of recreation and exercise. Frankly, it's 24-hour care.

Which all goes to say that I know we are on borrowed time here. I call Paddy my dog with nine lives. I think he's on seven. In the past year he's had several urinary infections, a variety of stomach ailments, and numerous glucose tests. By this time I could have paid for a new Mitsubishi.

And it's a good thing this deadline is just days before publication, 'cause between now and then anything can happen. So we're trying to be good sports around here. We lament having two dogs of roughly the same old age, but we try to keep our senses of humor at our canine assisted living facility.

I want to know whether we're eligible for respite care.▼

May 2012

It Gets Better than Better

I want to do one of those *It Gets Better* ads, telling our gay kids that not only does it get better, it can get freakin' fabulous.

For me, the past two weeks have been a tale of two cities, Rehoboth and New Orleans, awash in gay culture and energized by our community.

We made our annual trip to the Saints & Sinners literary conference in N'awlins and I'm surprised to report that we were slightly more saint than sinner this year, foregoing an excess of bar-hopping for rest and relaxation at the hotel pool.

On the town, we found making friends a snap. We hadn't been in the gayborhood five minutes, with our first Hurricanes placed on the bar before us, when a young man leaned over to me and said, "Drink your juice, Shelby." This steel magnolia, who uttered this signature line from *Steel Magnolias*, was from Texas and knew that line was universal gay speak. Before long we were buds, with plans to meet up the next night. I love our gay culture!

At dinner time, we found a restaurant without a liquor license which encouraged patrons to bring their own. We used our half hour wait for a table to amble to the gay bar down the block and order cocktails to go. I still smile every time I walk down a New Orleans street carrying a roadie.

"We need plastic cups, " I told the bartender, "We're taking them to dinner at the corner."

"Take a real glass, honey, have fun and return it later," came the reply. We took the finery, had the fun and returned the glasses later, along with having a wee nightcap (and this was our year to be less sinnerly!).

But all good things must end, so we arrived at the airport at noon Sunday to find our flight home viciously overbooked. We heeded the call for volunteer bumpees, rewarded by free round trip tickets to anywhere AirTran flies. Woo-Hoo!

The down side was spending the next seven hours trapped in the vicinity of Gate 16. There was nothing to do but eat and drink and listen to funky NOLA jazz on the airport speakers. Not so bad, actually. We spent our incarceration reading a little, but mostly chowing down on alligator sausage, po' boys, and the ubiquitous red beans and rice. Oh yeah, we met some other Friends of Dorothy on the concourse and had some laughs along with our copious Cajun cuisine. By flight time I feared our stomachs exceeded the size limit for carry-ons and we would be consigned to the baggage compartment.

We got home just in time to continue the over-indulgence on Rehoboth's much heralded Memorial Day weekend.

As I sat under an umbrella at the girl's beach, surrounded by thousands upon thousands of lesbians, I couldn't help thinking, probably for the zillionth time in the 18 years I've been enjoying that beach, about my good fortune.

If, when I was going through the teeth gnashing and angst of coming out, some 35 years before, somebody had told me I would someday be on a beach, with a great group of friends, surrounded by this many other lesbians, I would have told them they were effing crazy. But here we were. Not only does it get better, but it gets freakin' fantastic.

And I was thrilled to see the staggering number of young lesbians, poised to carry on Rehoboth's reputation as Gayberry RFD (even though they don't know the reference!) for generations to come.

A second weekend event found us at a block party amid a terrific crowd of folks, gay, straight, young, not-so-young, all enjoying the perfect weather and picnic buffet. One family had a keg in the backyard. Now I missed a lot of keggers back in the day, during my angst-riddled college years. As I pumped the keg's plunger and helped fill many a cup for my friends and myself, I saw the irony. Collecting Social Security and being at a keg party seemed perfectly compatible.

It was at the last event of the weekend where this It Gets Better tale peaked. Bon and I attended a big party at the home of women we've known casually, but not well. One of the hostesses caught me and Bon on our way out the door and told me the most amazing tale.

Her homophobic dad was forced by circumstances to come to live with her and her partner. It was tense and uncomfortable. But, in a chance encounter, one day, her dad found one of my books on the back of the porcelain horse in the, ahem, library, (which, I have always said is the perfect place for them, short chapters and all) and he began to read. He laughed a little, read a story or two about the consequences of homophobia, and then laughed a little again. After finishing the book, he had some questions, and his attitude about gays began to change for the better. He got better.

Now I don't know if I deserve all the credit the hostess bestowed, because I'm sure these delightful gals, in a loving and committed relationship, showed Dad the best of marriage equality for themselves. But the story made me proud that my long ago choice to write honestly, in the first person, telling about the fun as well as the frustrations of gay life in Rehoboth may have actually done some good. Hearing that I make people laugh is fun. Hearing that I make them understand, is extraordinary.

So if you know any tweens, teens, or young adults grappling with coming out or coming to terms with gender issues, or whatever else they may be grappling with on the continuum of GLBTQ whatever, tell them I said, "It gets better. And after that, it gets even better than better."▼

June 2012

Paddy Jacobs-Quesenberry, 13, passed away on Thursday, May 31, 2012 from complications of diabetes. Born on St. Patrick's Day 1999, he spent his career working as a cover model for A&M Books of Rehoboth. His photograph appeared on the covers of *As I Lay Frying—a Rehoboth Beach Memoir*, *Fried & True—Tales from Rehoboth Beach*, and *For Frying Out Loud—Rehoboth Beach Diaries* all by Rehoboth Beach writer Fay Jacobs.

Paddy is survived by his family, including Fay and Bonnie, his older brother Moxie, Aunt Gwen and 39 feline cousins, and best friends Mitzi Hooker and Chanel Sneider-Cohen.

• • •

When I wrote my column about Schnauzerhaven Assisted Living a short time ago, I had no idea this news would follow so soon. As I have many *Letters* readers who didn't get this news personally, I feel a responsibility to let you know, in this space, of Paddy's passing.

Also, it's a chance to reiterate my view of story-telling. As I have said before, I inherited a gift from my father. It was his vision that no event is so terrible if you can tell a funny story about it. In fact, laughter is the very best medicine.

So I have to relate that following our terrible trip to the vet on that sad Thursday night, Bonnie and I were a mess. But she had a previously planned trip out of town and I told her to go. I assured her Moxie and I would be fine.

As I sat in my living room on Friday, Moxie could not settle down. He went from room to room in the house, looking for Paddy. While it was breaking my heart, I realized he hadn't seen Bonnie since Thursday night either. My God, he probably thinks I killed them both.

Between laughing and crying, I got through the night.

Bonnie's back now, and we're adjusting. Moxie is feeling a

bit more secure and we've been taking him to friends' homes for play dates. Paddy lives on, his face gracing the covers of thousands of books at Proud, Browseabout, Amazon.com, Barnes & Noble, etc., but mostly in great big stacks in my garage. In his memory, buy a book...see, I can shamelessly turn everything into a marketing opportunity.

As for his super model career, photographer Murray Archibald always had less trouble posing Paddy than me. Unlike me, Paddy never whined that he'd rather the photos didn't highlight his thighs, never squinted unattractively into the camera and didn't come up with a dozen shots with his eyes closed. And goodness knows, he was not picky about which photos would make good cover shots.

So the smiles continue. Bonnie and I giggle that our kitchen floor no longer looks like Lake Superior. Paddy, it can now be told, had a drinking problem. He couldn't take a sip of water without sticking his entire beard in the bowl, then dripping all over the floor. Then wiping his disgusting beard on the sofa. We smile, remember, and feel hopeful for the longevity of our new couch.

Finally, this column would not be complete without a nod to the incredible compassion and wonderful care of Dr. Sarah Curtis at Rehoboth Animal Hospital. The whole office is amazingly friendly and efficient. Cannot recommend them enough.

Oh, and I know Paddy would want me to say, "In lieu of flowers, donations to Delaware ASPCA, please." Just kidding. No response required. But we do have to go on kidding. It is the best medicine of all.▼

June 2012

LAPPING THE TRACK ON EIGHT WHEELS AND A PRAYER

There could not have been two New York City episodes further separated in style and substance than the two I experienced a couple of weeks ago. That they both involved my idol Angela Lansbury is by turns odd and exhilarating.

First, for the sublime: I went to see the revival of Gore Vidal's *The Best Man*, a brilliant political drama taking place in the 1960s that is as relevant today as it was then. Scary. The smallest star role was Angela's as a flag-waving Southern political committee woman. She was, of course, charming, funny, and perfect. But the show's big attractions were James Earl Jones, John Larroquette, Eric McCormack and Candice Bergen, so how could the show have been anything but brilliant and electric? It was a theatre-lover's grand slam.

Then we moved from sublime to ridiculous: The Gotham Girls Roller Derby.

When I was told to wear closed toe shoes if I was going to sit in the front row for the grudge match between the Manhattan Mayhem and the Brooklyn Bombshells, I should have known better. Holy rollers!

The match took place in the gym at Hunter College in Manhattan, where hundreds and hundreds of fans piled in to watch their favorite teams skate it out. The all-women teams had both male and female cheerleaders, and the crowd was nothing if not freakily diverse. Young, old, gay, straight, cheering, and screaming for their favorite skaters.

The athletes, a combo of gay and straight it seemed, dressed in hottie outfits of scanty panties or bike shorts and long tees over black three-quarter tights, plus knee pads, elbow pads and helmets, transported themselves not on roller blades but on the old-fashioned four-wheel models. Pumping their arms, sometimes their chests, and flying around the track like lightning, it was a sight to behold…and to duck for cover from.

From the program: "The objectives of roller derby are relatively simple. Each team fields a single point scoring skater ("Jammer") whose object is to lap as many opposing skaters as they can. The remaining skaters who aren't scoring points work both on offense and defense at the same time—to block the opposing Jammer and to clear a path for their own Jammer. Well-played roller derby requires agility, strength, speed, control, peripheral vision, communication, and teamwork."

Also cursing, screaming, bleeding. I haven't seen such aggressive women since 1978 at the Phase One bar on 8th Street in DC. And the tattoos! There hasn't been so much ink since John Hancock wrote on parchment.

Every time the gals started a round (a jam), they'd whiz by so fast, first you'd get windburn, then be whipped silly by a tailwind. Round and round they'd skate, uttering taunts, maneuvering bodies, sly elbowing (Foul!) with order trying to be kept by a cadre of striped-shirted referees, mostly male. The penalty box was always, always full.

When somebody went down, lots of folks went down, with wheels spinning, women cursing, and fans cheering. It was less a blood sport than ice hockey, but not by much. The platoon of refs kept everybody pretty much in line.

I think the best part for me, was the roster. The skaters boasted names like Ann Phetermean, Bitch Cassidy, Megahurz, Raggedy Animal, and such for the Mayhem. The Bombshells had Amesto-Maim, Bonita AppleBomb, Violet Knockout, Ann Frankenstein, and, as a writer familiar with the printing biz, my favorite, Em Dash.

These powerfully built, strong, independent women obviously had a blast doing derby in big, bad New York and it was a hoot to watch.

Luckily, no personal podiatry was required as a result of my sitting right at the action. Each time the jammers and their entourage flew by, often within an inch or two of my shoes, I'd scrunch my feet back and pray. When a pile-up of sweaty, butch gals landed at my feet I didn't know, as they sort of say, whether to sit or go blind.

But when I came knees to knees with one particular skidding skater, my night was complete. Right there, practically in my lap, was Angela Slamsbury.

As the sign I saw on my way out of the city said, "If You Can Make It Here...You Really Should." From gritty political drama to death-defying roller derby, I was a great big part of it, New York, New York. ▼

June 2012

It's time to act our age at the beach. And since we're all responsible adults, we should just haul our bones to the beach, waddle onto the sand, relax quietly under an umbrella, stay away from junk food and go home early.

Really? I have come up with a new summer workout regimen. It's kind of a cross between slothery and enjoying what the beach has to offer. As Goldilocks would say, not too tough, not too easy, just right.

Walk & Reduce – I get an all-day parking pass for the neighborhoods, where feeding the hungry parking meters is not required. That way I am shedding calories by walking the few blocks to Rehoboth's commercial district and boardwalk. True, sprints to feed the ravenous meters are slimming, but fines for memory lapses only exercise my mouth and middle finger.

Bench Press – Since the backs on the historic white boardwalk benches flip from front to back, I can rest my glutes and watch the ocean for a while, then press the back of the bench and scoot it the other way. That's when I get to stare at the eternally amusing humanity. As my late father once said as I wheeled him down the boardwalk to enjoy the night air and the tourists, "If this is America, we're in trouble." Okay, the boardwalk at night is a little like the crowd at a state fair or Renaissance Faire, but what the heck. If I get up and down enough for food, drink, or to get a better view of something outrageous I have just witnessed, I can achieve my requisite squats.

Crunches – Oh, where to start? Caramel popcorn is the crunchiest, but beach fries come in second. On days I'm up to it I compete in the pizza, taffy, funnel cake triathlon. While I know stretching is key, I avoid holding a French fry aloft to the swooping gulls. Those beastly birds can hover and discharge simultaneously, requiring lunges just to duck and cover.

Balance – As in checkbook. Love exercising the debit card with retail therapy. In this arena I have real stamina. Sadly, I can easily spend 5K in 5K. But if I'm picky I can really stretch those dollars along with the hamstrings.

Cardio Workout – I'm off to Skee-Ball at the arcade, where just the right effort is required to win prize tickets but steer clear of rotator cuff issues. It's best to avoid hyperextension, meaning you have to bend down and rip the prize tickets off after every game, lest they extend to where other, more hyper players can steal them. The key is flexibility—be happy with the souvenir kazoo or the backscratcher.

Going for the Burn – With all this exercise it's time to relax, but I can still go for the burn on a blanket on the sand. This is a good place to do curls, as in curling up with a good book. Of course, actual burning is unwise, so I apply sunscreen, SPF 146 epoxy. Then I practice my resting heart rate.

Body Building – Using a plastic pail and shovel, I do aerobic sand sculpting, building shark and starfish bodies. Burying the occasional human in the sand is fun and is low impact as long as the person is willing to be buried.

Cool Down – Where else but in the ocean? I usually need a spotter for this activity to remind me to take off my expensive glasses first. This cool down phase can be exhilarating, but be warned, I have seen it turn into a 100-meter dash at a jellyfish sighting.

Strength Training – The evening exercise session is where I build endurance. I start with the 12-ounce Dogfish Head beer and toil my way up to the 18 ounce. I'm working on my six pack. Talk about ripped. An alternative is the antioxidant pomegranate martini. As in many exercise programs, prior carbohydrate loading may be required, giving me an upper body workout from fork lifting.

Dumbbell Time – This happens as I exit town, powerlifting my beach chair and purchases. I've forgotten where I parked. It's hell getting old.

Chin-ups – The car will surface eventually. It can't be far. And I live here. What can be better than that? Life's a beach and I can get right back onto this treadmill again tomorrow. As they say, chin up. All of them. ▼

Up the Lazy River Without a Paddle

I've been trying to stay cool, in every sense of the word. That's how I wound up one day at Jungle Jim's Waterpark in Rehoboth.

In the fourteen years since Jungle Jim's and I have both lived in Rehoboth, we had never met before. Sure, we glanced at each other as I passed along Route One, with me wondering who on earth would stand in line on a hot summer day just to be hurled down an aluminum tube to certain drowning.

But then a friend had what she thought was a splendid idea for belatedly celebrating my 64th birthday. I wasn't even done asking, "Are you insane?" when five of us were in bathing suits, heading for the apocalypse.

Entering the park, my companions suggested we relax first on the Lazy River. We rode on tubes, swept along a curving, meandering route by a surprisingly swift current. Along the circuit we dodged a couple of overhead waterfalls, 3-foot seas from the wave pool and intermittent unruly behavior by adjoining twelve year olds. We giggled and guffawed, completing the circuit twice. Although tempted, no pre-teens were harmed in the making of this journey.

At the exit steps, trying to get myself out of the unflatteringly spread-eagled position I'd assumed in the tube, I squiggled and scrunched, flopped into the water, and heard a loud and clear "pop" from the vicinity of my right hip.

Crap. I envisioned the headline "Woman breaks hip on Lazy River." Wanting to find out if I could stand, I stepped backward, got caught by the current, and was swept by the rip tide, tubeless, down river. Fighting the surge and squawking like a chicken I clung to the rock wall at the edge of the lazy good for nothing river, and struggled to get back the long six feet to the steps.

As panicked companions reached for me, I bobbed like Shelly Winters being extracted from the Poseidon's Lido Deck.

Back at the steps, I learned that yes, I could still walk, albeit with a great pain in my ass, literally.

Off we trudged to our next adventure, which in a 4-1 vote was the 5-person raft down the Stampede waterslide. Getting the five of us clowns into the Volkswagen raft created a bizarre tangle of legs and torsos, with me seated backwards, first to go down the chute. It didn't matter. I never opened my eyes.

Our overcrowded raft shot downhill on a hideously steep slope, careening at terrifying angles along the banked sides of the tube, crashing through walls of water and speeding dangerously toward oblivion. Yes, I reasoned, this raft was made for five people, but was it made for these five people? Would we be spit out the end, carom off the bottom to be launched over the bus station onto Route One? I don't think this is what the tourism folks had in mind with their Reach the Beach campaign.

Happily we landed in the water with no more than a thud and the humiliating prospect of untangling ourselves before a viewing public. I'm sure we were the biggest vessel to go down since Titanic. The lucky pair to dig out first voted our next activity to be the Anaconda slide, the most giant of all the giant slides. This time it was a two-person raft, for me and my spouse. I told the young person running the gig I had changed my mind and didn't want to go down. He clearly didn't want to hear me.

As he shoved us off, I spied the incredible roller coaster plunge we were about to take. I HATE roller coasters. My idea of a thrill ride is a BMW down Fifth Avenue. But down we plummeted, through stomach-dropping, screaming, Space Mountain corkscrew turns and then into massive, punishing walls of water. This was a roller coaster in a car wash and I was the bug on the windshield.

Then, air borne, we became Thelma and Louise. God I hated it.

Finally, the torture ended and we staggered back over to the Lazy River to decompress. This time en route I graciously ceded my position to a small child and wound up, like Niagara's Maid of The Mist, directly under a torrential waterfall. No harm, no foul compared to the punishing Anaconda tsunami.

And, I am loathe to admit this, at the end of my lazy journey, I needed the assistance of an 11-year-old Good Samaritan to help get my Orca butt out of the raft. But all's well that ends well. As for my end, well, my right cheek hurt for days.

But like zip-lining before this, I didn't exactly enjoy the water slides but I'm glad I did it. Frankly, I'm done proving I can keep up with my mate on these adventures. Next time I will turn the other cheek and cruise along in the BMW.

Wait! Did somebody just mention bumper cars at Funland? Well, maybe just one more adventure. Most of my discs aren't slipped...yet. ▼

SUNSET AT CAMPOBELLO

It was very nearly the perfect vacation. Maine lobsters, stunning Nova Scotia scenery, visiting the charming Prince Edward Island and a plan for our last three days on Campobello Island, off the coasts of Maine and New Brunswick.

Perfect is lovely for a vacation, unless of course, you are a writer with a deadline and perfect is, frankly, not that interesting. Face it, bad reviews are more fun to read than good ones; tragedy and comedy more compelling than, say, 300 pages of nice.

Ergo, I hoped for vacation column fodder. With my spouse driving and me riding shotgun in our behemoth RV with a Jeep hauled behind, me not the most avid camper and my mate not the most sympathetic to my anti-bug, anti-fresh air tendencies, there was great potential. But zilch, nothing. Nada. Oddly, I loved it all. Ah, the smell of Deep Woods Off in the morning.

I even took my paddle-phobic butt kayaking, fearful of capsizing, but half hoping drama would ensue. Hope floated. Nothing.

But just when it was safe to go back in the water, we snatched defeat from the jaws of victory. We tried to find Campobello Island. Franklin and Eleanor Roosevelt's summer home is now a museum there and I wanted to see it. That, and more stunning shoreline, lighthouses and lobster suppers.

The problem was, the shortest route from Canada was by two ferries, too small to handle our multi-vehicle traveling circus. We'd have to cross back into the U.S., drive another hour and reach the island via Maine's FDR Bridge. It sounded simple.

Instructing our GPS bitch on the dashboard to head for the FDR bridge, we set out around 6 p.m. However, without consulting us, the bitch determined the shortest route to be ferry to ferry, across the whole stupid island, accessing the bridge bassackwards, from its Campobello side. We're so used to trusting these electronic babysitters, we didn't wake up and smell the seagull poop until she had us in line for the first ferry.

"Back up!" shouted the ferry staff, only you can't back up an RV towing a car unless you enjoy seeing both vehicles in the body shop. Sadly, we know this first hand. So I had to get out, amid a swarm of monster mosquitoes and use tarmac hand signals to guide our personal parade in an ungainly u-turn on a skinny gravel path. Going off road, we trampled several medium sized trees, shot gravel at a dozen cars and lodged a sapling in our windshield wiper.

So now it's 7:15 and we relaunched for Maine. This time I told GPS smarty pants I was doing the recalculating and sent her to the border as a via point to the bridge.

We made it to customs, where, just as they had done when we entered Canada, the agents spent a lot of time discussing whether the amount of booze we were carrying was over the legal limit. It was a rare instance of wishing I drank more the night before.

Back in the U.S, all was well until we were instructed to veer off in a peculiar direction and dontcha know that bitch managed to lead us to the second ferry we wouldn't be allowed to board.

Passing a bank parking lot with wide berth for another outsized U-turn, we were fully committed before spying the canopy over the drive-in banking lane. Slamming the brakes caused a ten-wheel squeal, and I got out to check the clearance.

"Abort!"

We would have sheared off the RV roof and dumped it onto the Jeep. It's rare you get a second chance to destroy your two vehicles at once, but here we were again. I watched as the driver bumped our motorcade up over a steep curb, wobbled it across a stretch of rutted turf, then bounced it back down again. By this time I'd been surrounded by a swarm of black flies and the booze the feds worried about was probably mixed drinks.

Backtracking yet again, our convoy finally got going the right direction but the GPS swore we'd arrive six minutes earlier than the current time on my watch. We were in a time warp, juggling Atlantic and Eastern Standard time zones.

"Recalculating!!" said the GPS.

"Oh, no you don't!" screamed the driver, unplugging the bitch and flipping her to the back of the bus. "No more of your friggin' shortcuts!"

We'd been on the road almost four hours for what we thought would be under two. Let's do the time warp again. We still had an hour or two to go depending whether we believed the arrival estimate had been a U.S. or Canadian calculation.

Driver (trying to turn left, peering past me to see): "Anything coming?"

Me: "Christmas."

Driver: "Was I supposed to turn there?"

Me: "You know, being lost in an RV is better than being lost in a car. When you refuse to ask the gas station for directions we can just pull over, have nightcap and go to sleep."

Driver, glaring: "If we get there I'm buying a t-shirt. It will be a collector's item. Who the hell can find this place?"

Me: "By the time we do, it will be sunrise at Campobello." (GROAN)

Eventually the elusive bridge appeared. We crossed onto the island and immediately saw flashing lights. Customs, again. We'd crossed from Canada into Maine and now we were going back into New Brunswick, Canada.

Border Patrol: "Any pets with you?"

Me: "Not unless you count the two-pound mosquitoes in here."

Border Patrol: "Any guns?"

Me: "No, If I'd had one I would have shot myself by now."

Border Patrol: "How much liquor do you have aboard?"

Me: "Unfortunately, the same amount we had when we left your country several hours ago."

Luckily I wasn't taken into custody.

125

By this time it was either midnight at the oasis or 11 p.m. and we'd flashed our passports, revealed we were unarmed and dogless, and explained our stash of Johnny Walker and Absolut ad nauseam.

But we made it to Campobello. And if GPS girl had not gone rogue, and if we had not gone border hopping and time warping, the vacation would have been utterly perfect. And that would have been too nice for words. ▼

HAIR TODAY, GONE BY BRUNCH

The faces on the folks watching the "What's the Buzz" event at the CAMP Rehoboth Community Center last Sunday morning told the tale. With gritted teeth, apprehensive looks and pretty much abject amazement, they watched my mate Bonnie and four other courageous souls get their heads shaved to raise funds and awareness for Team Ted and the ALS Association.

The team's Ted is Ted Pokorny and his wonderful wife Jo. They have long supported Rehoboth causes large and small, so when Ted was diagnosed with Lou Gehrig's Disease—or ALS—their Rehoboth friends joined the fight.

Bonnie's mom had succumbed to the horrid illness, and one of our New York writer friends, the brilliant Bob Smith, is courageously fighting it, too. So Bonnie joined the team.

Come Sunday morning at the CAMP Rehoboth Community Center, the participants and peanut gallery gathered for the buzz off. Yes, it was shear madness.

Bryan Hecksher of Auto Gallery was the first to get the buzz, and his new bowling ball hairdo must have suited him, because he suddenly became all show biz, taking charge of the stage and beckoning Bonnie to be next. Up she went, and Bryan himself grabbed the scissors and went to work. Now I knew all her hair was eventually going to go, but it was still a little scary seeing a used car salesman, albeit an incredibly honest one, chopping away at my wife's locks.

After doing a bit of a comedy routine, Bryan relinquished the shears to a pro who had volunteered her time for the event. Within minutes, Bonnie's hairdo was down to a frightening 1980 Mullet. Good God, don't stop there! Bald is better.

Sure enough, next came the clippers and Bonnie, known for clipping a Schnauzer or two in her day, was getting the same kind of treatment. Canines all over the area could be heard snickering. From the Mullet, the hairdo degenerated into a kind of a Dykes on Bikes cut. Yuk.

The next to last stage was a Mohawk, which was kind of fun, but then it was quickly followed by complete baldness. Then came the ear jokes.

"Wow," Bonnie said, gazing into the mirror. "From the back I bet I look like a Volkswagen with the doors open."

"Or *Star Trek*'s Mr. Spock," I said. It's true, the ears stood out like billboards.

Pretty soon it was done. Bonnie's fear of revealing a lumpy head did not come to pass, and the buzz cut looked great— well, her head was bright white compared to her tanned face, and pretty much looked like it would glow in the dark, but otherwise the close shave looked good on her. Thank goodness she didn't wind up looking like that 70s detective Kojak.

As Bonnie stepped from the chair, some of my former friends, including my formerly much-loved state representative started chanting, "Fay! Fay! Fay!" I ran outside so quickly I almost landed in the courtyard foliage.

"I've never seen her move so fast in her life!" said the Speaker of the House.

I escaped for two reasons. First, this was Bonnie's gig. (Stop groaning and calling this an excuse!). She deserved the spotlight for her courage and commitment to the cause.

And second, I'm a complete chicken shit. There, I admit it. For me, this was a close shave indeed.

Overall, the willingness of these volunteers to set up the event and get buzzed is marvelous. As for my spouse, I have never been more proud of her. She's amazing.

Our local paparazzi had a field day snapping pix of Bonnie and the others posing with Ted and Jo, making shocked faces into the flashing cameras and making certain "What's the Buzz" was a huge success. They raised a lot of money and will continue to raise a lot of awareness and that's so very important.

As for my girl, I immediately found her some nice laaarge earrings, and ran to the Shirt Factory so they could make her a t-shirt saying "I Shaved My Head for ALS Awareness."

"Eeew," she said later, "It's still a little fuzzy. Here, feel."

I rubbed her scalp and it did feel a little like the fuzzy side of Velcro. I told her we could just attach the EZ Pass to her head and all she'd have to do at toll booths was lean forward.

Later that night she realized her head was cold and said, "I wish I had an old fashioned night cap to wear to bed."

I didn't have to wish. I went right to the bar and made myself one.▼

September 2012

This never would have happened with a roll of film. There would have been no Kodak moment with me crawling on my hands and knees, like a pig sniffing for truffles, hunting for a two gigabyte digital camera chip. No, this crisis is brought to you by Silicon Valley.

Bonnie, Moxie, and I visited friends in Maryland recently, where a new household member, a young Airedale named Benson, had Moxie's full attention. So enamored was senior citizen Moxie, that he ran alongside Ben, his inner puppy on display, for hours on end in the backyard. This fact is key, it comes up later.

Emmie the Cocker Spaniel joined Benson and Moxie, and photo ops of the bounding pooches abounded.

After taking three cute pictures and viewing them on the camera, I handing off the Sony Cybershot to my pal across the table. She immediately noticed the battery compartment flap open, and an empty slot where the photo chip should have been.

"It was there a minute ago," I said, "I just took pictures and saw the results."

Four minds with a single thought: "The chip fell out under the table, don't let one of the dogs eat it!" As I said, an old fashioned roll of Kodachrome would not have initiated this emergency.

Complete with synchronized groans and unfortunate forehead banging, the four of us dove under the table to search for the errant chip. Nothing. Thinking it might have fallen through the deck onto the gravel patio below, our quartet scurried down the steps to go beachcombing. Lousy on the knees and no success to boot.

Baffled and concerned, we went about our business for the rest of the day, stopping often to wonder exactly where the good chip lollipop had gone.

That night, Emmie suffered a bout of the trots and we were all certain she had ingested two gigabytes of memory and its surrounding plastic, metallic, industrial strength parts. By the next day, a veterinary visit, complete with intestinal x-ray, revealed no foreign bodies in her system and she was diagnosed with garden variety stomach trouble. Perhaps it was too many table scraps, the heat, or the excitement of a new Airedale in the house. But it took $165 at the vet to declare the Maltese Chip's whereabouts still a mystery.

Meanwhile, back at our ranch, Moxie refused to get out of bed, and when he did, he shuffled like comic Tim Conway's Mr. Tudball on the old *Carol Burnett Show*. And if you remember that, you probably once had a chipless Brownie Starflash camera, too.

Poor Moxie. Something seemed really wrong. He had to have swallowed the missing chip. We kept looking for him to produce, um…evidence we could reluctantly examine, but none at all was forthcoming.

In fact, he had not produced any evidentiary material at all in twenty four hours. Naturally, he waited until 3 a.m. the following night to let us know exactly how sick he was. He wouldn't settle down, and was whimpering in pain. Good thing we now have an emergency vet clinic right up the street. Damn Cybershot. What I wouldn't give for my Kodak pocket camera with the 110 cartridge. Nobody could have swallowed that hunk of junk.

Examinations and x-rays ensued, as we explained our fear that somewhere in Moxie's digestive system, there lurked a two gigabyte memory chip recording his stomach contents. The young vet tech looked at me blankly when I joked that this could not have happened if I still used my Instamatic camera with flash cubes.

"Flash cubes?" she said, as if I had mentioned rotary phones or Green Stamps.

No intestinal chip. Moxie, it turns out was seriously constipated, requiring a "procedure." Four hundred and twenty dollars later, the middle-of-the-night doggie enema complete, the vet had a theory. She believed that elder statesman Moxie romped with his doggie pals so energetically that he was quite the hurting puppy—and bending his knees to "assume the position" in the back yard was too painful for him to bother. So he didn't. Made sense to me.

As for goodbye mister chip, two weeks later, I was sitting at my desk, when I glanced over at the printer.

There, sticking out of the camera chip slot was, surprise, a camera chip. What the hell? If the chip was there all the time, and never in the camera, how did I take the pictures of the romping canines?

I learned that digital cameras have hard drives and they can take a couple of photos without any memory chip at all. Who knew? So we never had a chip in the camera in the first place, it never fell out, we never had to play Sherlock Holmes, we needn't have worried about our dogs' colon health and I feel like a complete chip off the old blockhead.

I want my Brownie Starflash back. ▼

THE EYES HAVE IT

As hairdresser Truvy says in *Steel Magnolias*, "Time marches on, and it's marching right across my face."

There's nothing like reading your medical chart and seeing the words Senile Optical Sclerosis. Good God! Never mind that SOS is just doctor speak for garden variety cataracts. The word senile evokes hysteria in me. This cannot be happening.

My last two months have been completely absorbed with cataract removal, first the right eye, then, four weeks later, the left. Within hours after the first surgery, I could see better than I had in years. I couldn't believe my eye.

Now, there's good news and bad news from this easy and painless surgery. The good news is that I can see clearly now, the rain is gone. But that's also the bad news. I looked in the mirror and shrieked. This wasn't just a new wrinkle, but dozens of them. I looked like a Shar Pei. Frankly, it wasn't all that bad spending years seeing myself like Doris Day filmed through gauze.

And worse, there on my neck, I spied a thick brown hair lengthy enough to tie in a sailor's knot. How long had that been there? And it had the gall not to turn grey like the stuff on my head. Irony.

Then came the eye drops. Four kinds, four times a day, although asking me to remember anything four times a day is cruel. I was always forgetting and dropping them in my eyes on my way out the door, so I'd arrive places looking like I was grieving. Only for my lost youth.

Bonnie often helped with the eye drop regimen, which after many weeks got a little old. Sometimes it recalled play-wright Neil Simon's line from *Plaza Suite*, where E.G. Marshall, getting eye drops, hollered to Maureen Stapleton, "You drop them in, you don't push them in!" Just kidding. I was the one more likely to stab myself in the eyeball.

Furthermore, the surgery rendered my $600 progressive lens, transition-coated eye glasses completely worthless. Sadder yet, I still need reading glasses and sun glasses but must wait over a month for my new prescription. For now I just juggle drug store readers and those bulky plastic sun glasses that go over the reading glasses. Now I'm Mr. Magoo. And whatever glasses I need are in the other room or the other car or nowhere at all until somebody points out that I have three pairs of ugly spectacles dangling from my shirt collar.

If the eye thing wasn't annoying enough, since July I've had the honor of being my physical therapist's first Jungle Jim water park injury. I popped a ligament from my hip to my knee squirming out of an inner tube back around July 4th on the Lazy River and walking has caused fireworks ever since.

For pity's sake, they should just put me up on blocks in the garage. I don't know whether to shit or go blind but I guess I can decide after my upcoming gastroenterologist appointment and eye doctor follow up.

By this time, I'm feeling older than dirt and quite disgusted, channeling Bette Davis' quote "Getting old is not for sissies." But sitting in the therapist's waiting room I read about the Wings and Wheels Fall Festival at the Georgetown Airport. It sounded like fun.

So early last Saturday morning, Bonnie and I ventured out to the airpark at Georgetown and signed up for biplane and helicopter rides. While we waited, we got to talk with a still-spry 90-year old about his days as a World War II bomber navigator and went to check out hundreds of antique cars. I was thrilled to see a classic 1964 Corvette, a model I owned for the decade between 1968 and 1978.

As for the rides, Bonnie went up in an open cockpit bi-plane, doing dips and turns and having a blast. I chose the helicopter ride, taking off over farmland and ocean, seatbelted into a see-through vehicle without doors. I loved it.

I'm happy to report that I didn't have too much trouble climbing in and out of the vehicle and the view with my new non-Senile-Optical-Sclerosis eyes was absolutely and utterly fantastic. Like that '64 'Vette, I felt classic, not antique.

Maybe what's been lovingly said about us gay people is true. We may get older, but thank goodness we never mature. I'm workin' it.▼

HEALTH INSURANCE: MAY THE FARCE BE WITH YOU

Last November I faced mission impossible—finding an affordable health insurance policy in the scant few months before becoming Medicare eligible.

Now I am not a wagering person. But stunned by the uber-pricey monthly premium quotes, I was forced to consider an uncharacteristic bet. I applied for a catastrophic policy, with the first $7500 of medical bills on me for December 2012 and then again, on me, when the deductible re-set, January-May, 2013.

Ha! I said to my spouse. I'm fine. If I accrue $15,000 worth of medical bills in the next six months we'll be in more than financial trouble. I'll take this catastrophic policy and keep the premium to a minimum.

The following day helped convince me I'd made the correct decision. First came an interminable afternoon answering intimate medical questions posed by a clueless clerk in Mumbai.

That was followed by a rowdy night playing the parlor game Minute to Win it. Geezer applicant by day, preschooler by night.

The day game saw me quizzed by a variety of non-medical personnel, hoping to declare me a medical disaster, all for the purpose of inflating my monthly premium. The clerk kicked off the inquisition.

"You saw a doctor for chronic Bronchitis?"

"No, I had Bronchitis once in 2009."

"How long have you had asthma?"

"I don't have asthma."

"But you have been prescribed an inhaler?"

"Yes, for the four days of Bronchitis, four years ago."

"So it is not chronic? Not ongoing?"

"Only the questions about it."

"Say yes if you have ever had the following diseases. Apnea, appendicitis, lupus, stroke, irritable bowel…"

"Just irritable applicant."

"Oh, ha-ha, you made a joke…leprosy, joint disease, rosacea, spinal tingling, rotator cuff problems, toenail fungus, sciatica…"

"z-z-z-z-z"

"I see you take cholesterol medicine, so I will check High Cholesterol."

"No don't, it's not high, now that I take a pill, it's low."

"So yes, I will check high cholesterol."

"Are we speaking English here?"

"And you were hospitalized with chest pain? A heart attack?"

"No, it turned out to be indigestion. Thai Food."

"Typhoon? What is that?"

"No, Thai…oh never mind."

"So no heart attack?"

"No, just gas. Which turned into a bit of a typhoon, actually."

The humorless solicitor continued.

"And what of this eye surgery? Was it a disease?"

"Yes, too many birthdays. I had a cataract removed and now I can see better than I want to. I screamed when I first looked in the mirror. I need a Lifestyle Lift."

By this time I'd used all my phone's anytime minutes and the call center guy was still probing. In the end, he passed me to a supervisory inquisitor, who announced they'd factor my "respiratory "and "coronary" risks into the monthly premium and get back to me. Fear of that final number did cause spinal tingling.

Following this phone marathon, we spent an evening with friends, including a game of Minute to Win It – baby-boomers, fueled by wine, doing stupid things. Not one to volunteer for humiliation, I resisted the game at first, but caved when one of the scenarios included Peanut M&Ms. I have my price.

There were two adjacent picnic tables. Following directions, I sat at a table in front of a cup of M&M Peanut candies. I was told to put a straw in my mouth, suck up an M&M and keep it dangling on the end of the straw while I got up and transported the inhaled trophy to a paper cup on the other table. I had one minute to see how many candies I could relocate.

Here's the thing. Instead of quizzing me about foot fungus and respiratory issues, my friend from Mumbai could have just watched me handily suck up the M&Ms (no asthma), painlessly untangle my aging knees from the picnic bench (no joint problems), keep those candies hanging by sheer lung power (no bronchitis) and deposit them neatly in their target cup (good eyes). Unlike our former president, I did inhale. Well enough, it turns out, to win the game over some younger contestants.

Next, somebody balanced a shortbread cookie on my upturned forehead, offering instructions to get the morsel to my mouth without using my hands. Hey, insurance geek, by wiggling all my vertebrae, I carefully jiggled a Lorna Doone down to my right eyebrow (no spinal tingles or whiplash), flipped it onto my eyelid (now there's a cataract) and gymnastically juggled it into to my mouth. Consuming my prize did not measurably inflate my cholesterol.

For the last game we blew up balloons, then used the balloon's escaping hot air to noisily propel a paper cup across a finish line. The impolite sound of the balloons in action brought back memories of the Thai food typhoon, which was not, I repeat not, a coronary incident.

Oh, and despite how much wine I consumed that night, my liver is just fine, too, thank you very much. Bring on the insurance premiums. I know the monthly bill will surely suck, whether I can inhale a one-pound bag of chocolate candies or not. But hell, it's just a stop-gap measure. Six short months. I intend to relax, stay away from doctors, take two M&Ms and pay the bill in the morning.

EPILOGUE

May the farce be with you. Not 24-hours after paying my first catastrophic insurance premium, catastrophe struck. (see following column). Yes, I wagered and lost. But I'm here to tell the tale and I still have enough hot air to suck a mean M&M Peanut. Medicare—coming soon to a writer near you.▼

February 2013

So here's the sad tale. My winter folly began innocently enough, one mid-November evening as I drove my beloved, geriatric BMW convertible on Route One. Now I'd like to tell you exactly what happened next, but I have no idea. I've been told that two cars, one being mine, merged simultaneously onto the same stretch of pavement. If I knew the details I'd know whether to be pissed off or guilty, but no such luck.

The luck was saved for me, for after a bounce, crunch, and an oddly slow motion impact, I said to myself, "Wow, that was a mess, but I'm fine."

I reached for my phone, pushed the button for home, and said to my spouse, "I've had an accident in front of China Buffet, I'm fine, but come get me." Then I dialed 911.

The following few minutes are lost in space, but the 1993 tank I hit or hit me (Buick? Olds? Titanic?) sat smashed against my driver side door, and its driver, who said she was fine, refused to move it until the police arrived to investigate. By the time Bonnie and some friends showed up I was still behind the wheel in a stupor.

As Bonnie poked her head in the passenger door I was struck by an adrenalin rush, causing me to boost my fat butt up over the gear shift, flip my legs up onto the windshield, and propel myself sideways out the passenger door like some Eastern European gymnast.

"I'm fine, I'm fine," I hollered to no one in particular as I executed an ungainly dismount. Bonnie gently said, "Look at your hand." Ewwww. It looked like a deep purple baseball mitt with a lump the size of a softball atop it.

Amid my moronic protestations of fineness, Bon ordered me to sit/stay on the curb and wait for the ambulance, which, in turn, hauled me off to the ER. There, I was assessed by a team of nurses and docs, sent to x-ray, and treated with extreme nurturing.

Turns out I broke pretty much every bone in my left hand.

"Anything else hurt?" they asked.

"Nope," I said, confidently.

While the team installed a temporary cast on my hand, a nurse tried to distract me from the pain.

"Are you still working or retired?" she asked.

"I'm retired."

"That's nice, how long have you been retired?"

"Twenty-five minutes."

And so it was. I went home with my paw in a sling, swallowed some industrial strength pain meds and fell asleep.

Now here's the interesting part. I awoke to discover I couldn't walk. I was unable to put any weight at all on my right knee and I was in excruciating pain. What the…???

Turns out I was a victim of a cognitive brain syndrome, where intense pain can only be perceived by the brain at one site at a time. Who knew? Well now I did. Not only was my hand broken, but later that day an MRI revealed a complex meniscus tear in my knee. So much for being fine. I wondered whether the knee injury was achieved on impact or from my compulsory gymnastics routine on exit.

One week later I had three hours of surgery to put together the jigsaw puzzle that was formerly my left hand, followed several weeks later by knee surgery. In fact, I had knee surgery on the predicted December 21 Mayan Doomsday, figuring if the worse were to happen, I'd be under anesthetic and go quietly for once.

So I spent the holiday season ensconced in my living room recliner, holding the ice bag on my swollen right knee with my swollen left hand, for a two-for-one. Too dopey from drugs to read or write, I mostly watched television. If *Honey Boo-Boo* doesn't foreshadow the end of civilization, perhaps *Storage Wars* does. However, I do think *Super Nanny* should be shown in high schools. One episode of shrieking, manic children and teens, would keep their panties on and zippers up.

A charming surprise was that Kelly Ripa and Michael Strahan are actually wicked smart and hilariously funny, a perfectly matched odd couple and a pleasure to watch. I atone for being previously dismissive of them.

In hand therapy they asked my goals and I said I lived to be able to flip the bird once again and, of course, type with more than two fingers. Several weeks into therapy I could press the keyboard shift button with my index finger. Ladies and gentlemen, we have achieved CAPITALS.

Then came the really bad news. The insurance company totaled the BMW. Like the character of Eponine in Les Miz, she gave her life for me. For a long time, shards of the sea green left front panel sat in a pathetic pile along the side of Route One, a make-shift shrine. One of my artsy friends offered to scoop them up and make a mobile for me, but by the time we got organized, somebody's trash service had eliminated the option.

By the end of December, Bonnie had been cheerfully channeling Clara Barton and Julia Child for six weeks and our friends had gone wonderfully wild on both casserole duty and ferrying me to and from therapy while Bonnie worked. For me, being stuck in the house unable to drive, type, tie my shoes or even put a brassiere on by myself was abject torture. Required meds precluded martinis and I was insane.

But by Christmas Eve, the turn-around began. I was mobile enough to go out dining and visiting. I made it to the New Year's Eve Gayla, even if I didn't make it to midnight. And a week later I walked to my neighborhood stop sign.

All in all, things are looking up. Yes, the Beamer is gone. But the knee is healed and the hand is improving. In fact, with this column, I surprised myself by typing again on all cylinders. And yes, despite the splint still on my hand, I can flip the bird, which I do several times a day while watching Congress on C-SPAN.

Oh, and except for my writing, I really did retire. So did Bonnie. And we're in Florida for a couple of weeks as you read this. Some events just put things in proper perspective.▼

VACATION OR RETIREMENT?
THAT IS THE QUESTION.

My mate and I just launched our retirement. There was a very un-beach like forecast of snow on the way as we bid a fond farewell to Rehoboth and set out along the Delmarva Peninsula, heading for Florida.

Much like a vision of the *Beverly Hillbillies* (if this reference means nothing to you, you are eons from retirement), our car was stuffed with suitcases, dog bed, dog bowls, portable dog crate, golf clubs, and a valise full of drugstore items from Prilosec to Sunscreen 70 Epoxy.

"Is this retirement or vacation?" I pondered aloud as we headed for the Bay Bridge-Tunnel.

With the brassy tune "The Stripper" playing in my head, we shed our outer garments one state at a time, with the coats gone by Virginia, the Rehoboth sweatshirt by South Carolina, and our sleeves rolled up by that night when the lights went out in Georgia.

As we explored Florida's West Coast, from St. Pete to Naples, we joyously watched the Weather Channel report on the blowing snow and frigid temperatures at home. At lunch one day, dining with friends on their lanai, enmeshed in excellent conversation (vacation?), we heard the splash. My 15-year old Schnauzer Moxie had waddled off the edge of the pool and sank like a gangster in cement shoes.

Frantic pushing and shoving ensued as four retirees struggled to get off our butts and race to the pool. The fittest of us leapt down the steps, into the water, and pulled the mutt from the depths. Happily, he was fine, if a little surprised, but requiring no mouth to snout CPR.

"Wow, that was lucky," gasped the first responder, "Ordinarily I would have had my iPhone in my pocket."

"If I had gotten there first, I *would* have had my phone in my pocket," I said.

"If you had gotten there first," said my spouse, "we would have phoned the scoop to the *New York Times*." So this is retirement. 24/7 with my spouse the comic.

The next day, we headed out to cross the Southern portion of the state, through the Everglades, along a route called, appropriately, Alligator Alley.

Inside the car, the vacation vs. retirement debate proceeded. After decades of punching the snooze button for ten more minutes before long, frantic work days, the delightful reality of retirement was upon us. In fact, we were so deep in our glee that we missed the last gas station before Alligator Alley and forgot to fill up.

Naturally, the moment we hit that spot when it was no longer possible to U-turn, the laughing yellow low fuel light popped up on the dashboard. To make matters worse, we were in a new car, with no knowledge of whether the light was a gentle suggestion or a Category 5 warning.

Idiots. We were trapped on Alligator Alley, gas gauge on empty and green-brown alligators staring longingly at us from roadside creeks. Okay, there was a fence between us and the gators' jaws, but walking for help alongside beasts of the Southern wild was not on my bucket list.

Should we drive at exactly 55 mph to preserve gas, but prolong the agony, or speed up to see how far we'd get before tragedy struck? The GPS advised that the only gas station before our Ft. Lauderdale destination was 42 miles away at an exit at Snake Road. Somehow, not all that comforting.

"Don't panic," said the driver. "We have Good Sam Roadside Assistance."

Really, out here? I guessed we'd get to see just how good Good Sam actually was.

Suddenly, I was oddly ambivalent. This fuel emergency might be a double edged sword. I hoped to make it to the filling station before wrestling gators, but driving that far with the gas light on meant a disquieting future.

How annoying would it be, when forevermore, I would suggest filling up at a quarter tank, with my spouse laughing and recalling running on empty through the Everglades?

By the time we rolled off at Snake Road, both the dog and I were panting and drooling, the alligators were pissed they'd missed lunch and the driver was grinning like a Cheshire Cat.

So we avoided catastrophe and made it to Ft. Lauderdale. Contrary to what we were afraid we'd find in Southern Florida (nickname: God's Waiting Room), we found the nightlife, they like to boogie. Lauderdale and Pompano Beach rocked, with plenty of entertainment, good restaurants and gorgeous beaches. If Rehoboth is Ying, Lauderdale is Yang.

So we've decided that until global warming turns Rehoboth Beach into Savannah, we will interrupt our beach retirement each winter for a Florida vacation.

On the return trip, we stopped in the South Carolina Low Country for a night in Beaufort (vacation), hoping we could stretch our funds just a little further to pay for the hotel (retirement). We took one of those wonderfully cheesy horse and buggy rides around the historic town to view its ante-bellum mansions and shrimp boat-filled harbor (vacation). After a feast of greasy fried shrimp, grits and hush puppies, we headed back to the motel for Prilosec and bedtime (retirement).

Back on the road in the morning, I asked a question and was immediately rewarded by my worst fear.

"Aren't you stopping for gas before getting onto I-95?"

"Pshaw. If we had enough in the Everglades..."

Back in Reho, as we did the mountain of laundry we had created, and looked at trip expenses on our Visa card, vacation quickly became plain old retirement. But frankly, both are pretty darn good. Every night is Friday night, every day is Saturday morning. Ahhhhh.▼

THE TIMES THEY ARE A-MAZ-IN'

Change is happening, kids!

Just this morning, Bonnie and I sat at the dining room table and both of us signed a single Delaware State tax return. As a civil unioned couple, we filed jointly. Woo-Hoo! Things really are changing.

In fact, just this week, the AP Stylebook, the bible for journalists and editors, etched into type the following rule: **husband, wife** — *Regardless of sexual orientation, husband or wife is acceptable in all references to individuals in any legally recognized marriage. Spouse or partner may be used if requested.*

Remarkable. But, just as striking are the things that aren't happening.

A few weeks ago Bonnie and I stopped for dinner and an overnight in Beaufort, S.C. (that's pronounced Bufort, not Bowfort) on our way home from Florida. We'd heard it was a charming historic town, a mini-Charleston, and surely worth a visit.

As I made dinner reservations, I realized our visit would coincide with Valentine's Day. Ding, ding, ding! Thirty years of alarm bells kicked in, making me wonder if a romantic dinner for two lesbians in South Carolina was advisable, or even safe. But I pushed through the residual fear and forged ahead.

On Valentine's morning we walked along the water admiring the flotilla of shrimp boats, moss-covered trees, and exquisite antebellum mansions. At lunchtime we ducked into a small restaurant and ordered low country specialties like oysters and hush puppies. As we waited for our meals, I mentioned to Bonnie that my left hand, still recovering from that accident last fall, was less swollen every day.

"Look," I said, offering her my two hands for comparison, "I'm starting to have visible knuckles again."

"That's great," she said, holding my hands in hers, studying the difference between the two.

When the young waiter returned and saw Bonnie lovingly holding my outstretched hands he did not, as might have happened years ago, avert his eyes and walk into a wall. Instead, he smiled and asked if we wanted to order a bottle of wine. Frankly, I'm glad he thought it was a romantic moment instead of an orthopedic exam.

We took an afternoon horse and buggy ride throughout the historic district, then set out for our Valentine's Night dinner. Would we be laid low in the Low Country? After 15 years of absolute diversity and comfort in Rehoboth, it was very odd worrying once again about how people would react to our same-sex coupleness. It was, after all, Valentine's Day in a bright red state, home of the late, hate-filled Senator Strom Thurmond.

I'm thrilled to report we had pointless angst. Dinner was lovely. The other patrons smiled at us, and we at them, as we all dunked bananas and pound cake in our Valentine's chocolate fondue. The screech from the kitchen might not have been the dish washer operating, but could as easily have been hate-monger Strom spinning in his grave.

After Florida we headed to NYC to visit friends and family. Standing across from Sardi's at Shubert Alley, all we could see were billboards for upcoming gay-themed shows. *The Nance*, stars Nathan Lane as a gay British Music Hall performer; *Kinky Boots*, a blockbuster musical by Cyndi Lauper and Harvey Fierstein is about a family shoe business saved from financial ruin by their willingness to make boots for drag queens; and the hottest of the hot shows. *The Book of Mormon* musical, with its gay themes, and a gay lead character, might just make it the gayest show on Broadway. The only hetero-centric billboard in sight was *Annie*, and we really have no idea about the dog's orientation.

Later, in Soho at a new women's bar, The Dalloway (a nod to Virginia Woolf), we found an upscale establishment in an uber-trendy neighborhood, with an elegant and well-lit sign. We heard that one of the owners is a former *America's Top Model* contestant. It's a far cry from the days when you needed a bodyguard to get you to or from a dimly lit, seedy watering hole in the worst part of town. It was a really far cry from the days when you might have needed the bodyguard inside the bar, as well.

Of course, as grateful as I am for the improvements, we ain't done yet. Equality Delaware is hard at work enlisting Delawareans to help get marriage equality before the legislature in Dover. And I am joining forces with them to direct the play *8*, in Rehoboth. It's the story of California's hateful Proposition 8 against gay marriage. We're doing a staged reading of this marvelous play, with local and professional actors to help raise funds for Equality Delaware.

And the sinister Proposition 8 itself, which has been declared unconstitutional in the lower courts, is set to go for oral argument before the U.S. Supreme Court in two weeks on Tuesday, May 26. If overturned, there can be marriage equality in California.

More importantly, the next day, March 27, Bonnie and I will celebrate our 31st Anniversary, and the one-year anniversary of our big fat Jewish Civil Union held at CAMP Rehoboth. This March 27, as fate would have it, the Supreme Court will hear the oral argument in the case of Edith Windsor v. The United States.

Eighty-three year old Edie Windsor is suing to overturn The Defense of Marriage Act (DOMA). She was outraged and offended, not to mention punished financially by having to pay a huge inheritance tax on her own home after her partner died. A surviving partner in a heterosexual marriage would not have had to pay the bill.

If DOMA is overturned, the U.S. government would have to recognize same sex marriages in states which allow it, and further, provide federal benefits and tax breaks—over 1000 benefits we do not now enjoy—to same sex married couples in those states. Huzzah!!!

Therefore, Bonnie and I will be with the throngs who intend to march on, picket, and otherwise storm the U.S. Supreme Court on Tuesday, March 27. We will loiter before the court building, carrying a sign reading:

**If Gay Marriage were LEGAL
today would be our 31st Anniversary!**

I hope we wind up in the Washington Post, or on Film at 11. 'Cause we ain't done yet.▼

March 2013

I don't have to run away to join the circus, it's in my house. And last night under the big top, I tried to be ringmaster but wound up in clown pants.

We babysit dogs. Last evening the census included my elderly Schnauzer Moxie, my friend's elderly Schnauzer Mitzi and an adolescent three-legged Yorkie we'll call Houdini—he has an uncanny ability to escape his confines better than any four-legged, or for that matter, two-legged creature I know.

Given the age and infirmity of the Schnauzers, plus the orthopedic disability of the Yorkie, you'd think the house would be a canine assisted living facility. But no, it's a cross between a maximum security prison and the greatest show on earth.

In deference to Houdini, we've erected a series of barriers to the front door. They include deadbolt lock-down at all times, a sturdy baby-gate crossing the hallway and, to be extra safe, a complex defensive running play at the sound of somebody ringing the bell. We start with room to room hollering, tap a player to run the Houdini Hail Mary forward pass to deposit him in the bathroom, then finally answer the door looking like we've run a 5K. The UPS guy thinks we're growing weed, or running numbers in here.

When we're home alone, the front door is the forbidden zone as we sneak out of our own house through the garage just to get the mail. Every time I walk to my den I have to jump the hallway hurdle, making the same sound my father used to make getting out of a chair.

We don't even trust Houdini in our fenced yard. One time he squeezed through the lattice work around the deck for an excursion of the murky under-deck mud flats. He sniffed his way through the three foot high deck, then slithered under a lower section, crawling on his belly like an infantryman. Unable to turn around, he got stuck. We heard the plaintive bark from under the boards and had to dismantle part of the deck to extricate Dora the Explorer. From that moment on, we kept Houdini on a short leash, even in the fenced yard. He now pees on a leash. Well, not *on* the leash, *while* on the leash.

So okay, last night started well enough, with mostly-deaf, mostly-blind Mitzi on the bed, along with a snoring Houdini. Mostly blind-mostly deaf Moxie was in his snuggly bed at the foot of ours. But at 5 a.m. Moxie got up. Once I hear his tags rattling I know I have about a minute to grab him, run out the back door, carry him down the two steps and deposit him in the grass before something happens involuntarily. For the trip, I generally like to add slippers and flannel pajamas to my tee-shirt ensemble, especially when it's 36 degrees out.

So there I am, at 5 in the morning, addled and barely conscious, putting two feet into one pajama leg, hopping around, trying to get my slippers on and get out before the waterworks. Houdini hears the ruckus, flies through the air with the greatest of ease and wakes Mitzi. Ergo, on our way out, Moxie and I have a thundering posse. Naturally, it's backyard chaos as I deposit Moxie before he makes a deposit, try to keep Houdini from diving under the deck, make sure Mitzi Magoo doesn't hurt herself bumping into the side of the glass door that isn't open. I don't suppose little window decals of Milk-Bones would help her distinguish the correct egress.

I wrangle all three pups back in and it's circus time as canines circle the living room, nose to butt, much like parading elephants. When Moxie wants breakfast, it's time to thin the herd.

I grab Houdini, run him to the bedroom, toss him onto the sleeping person, and close the door behind me. From the giggling of my now-awake mate, I know I've failed and the three-legged sprinter is already back in the kitchen. As P.T. Barnum once said, there's a sucker born every minute.

I make Moxie's meal, set it down, turn my back to get Mitzi's food, and Houdini sticks his snout in Moxie's bowl. Once again I pick him up, go to the bedroom, hand him off to the laughing person, and go back out. Houdini's incarcerated, but now Mitzi's eating Moxie's food. I move Mitzi to a spot in the corner and yell "Stay!" As Moxie heads to his bowl, Houdini's back, having used one of his remaining limbs to open the bedroom door. I put him in an opposing corner and holler "Stay!" Nobody listens. Done playing Siegfried and Roy, I just put three bowls of gruel down and let them all have at it.

By this time it's 5:15 a.m. and two humans and three dogs are all wide awake. Houdini does his high wire act hopping along the back of the sofa, and the other two are butt to butt in one tiny bed. Step right up ladies and gentlemen to our circus sideshow where we have the amazing two-headed Schnauzer.

Naturally, by sunrise at Attica, the three dogs have settled into the sofa, all sound asleep. The humans swig coffee and are reduced to watching infomercials. I look down to see that my slippers are on the wrong feet and my pajama bottoms are inside out. Send in the clown.▼

March 2013

Dammit. We had to put Moxie down today after a glorious 15 years.

He was sick and in pain and it was the right thing to do, although we are terribly sad and missing him like crazy. At the moment and for the future, at least in the short term, this house is no longer a Schnauzerhaven.

Well traveled, Moxie toured Maine and Nova Scotia by RV, I-95 to Florida and back and many other destinations. He loved the book *1000 Places to Pee Before You Die*, (seriously, it's a real book written by a Schnauzer). He did his best.

He was predeceased by his brother Paddy. He leaves his niece Margo Peterson and best friends Mitzi Hooker, Toddy Simmons-Thompson, Chanel Cohen-Sneider, Cleo & Lizzie Martinucci-Kozey, old man Atticus, and many, many more good friends, canine, feline and human.

It was a great run. And we will now be able to put the toilet paper on the holder instead of up on a shelf to prevent his unrolling it throughout the house. ▼

April 2013
A Sign of the Times for Marriage Equality

Sometimes I think the pace with which the gay marriage debate has overtaken the country has been achingly slow and other times it feels like an overnight sensation.

On Wednesday, March 27th, as Bonnie and I stood on the steps of the Supreme Court, oral arguments for overturning the Defense of Marriage Act (DOMA) raging inside, it felt like both. On one hand, after marching, joining gay rights organizations and donating money for the cause for over thirty years, I was amazed that the U.S. Supreme Court was finally discussing the matter; on the other hand, I couldn't believe I'd see this day in my lifetime.

Also, I was laughing. First, we'd bundled up and schlepped from our hotel to the court on foot—about a mile—and I was pleased to do it.

Second, we forgot to put slits in our four-foot sign proclaiming **If Gay Marriage Were Legal, Today Would Be our 31st Anniversary**, so the windy conditions turned the sign into a giant sail. I hoped we wouldn't be carried aloft to land in the midst of the pitifully small Westboro Baptist Church contingent. If, as they say, God hates Fags, they'd really hate me and Bonnie landing on them like some flying house from Oz.

Thirdly, our people in front of the court were nothing if not clever and colorful. Favorite signs included **Three Words to Fix the Economy: GAY BRIDAL REGISTRY, Get out of your DOMA Coma**, and the humble **My Sexuality Doesn't Define Who I Am, but I Sure Am Fabulous!**

Early in the morning, Bonnie and I had a choice to make. We could stand in the long, long line for those waiting to get into the court for a three-minute walk-through, or just stay outside with the supportive throng. We chose the open air option and it was a great choice.

From the minute we stepped in front of the court and unfurled our sign, and for three hours following, we stayed busy, being interviewed by the likes of Reuters, Newsweek, NPR, NBC, AP and dozens more. Cameras and cell phones flashed in our faces, giving us a delicious taste of paparazzi life.

Reactions to our sign ranged from "cool" with a thumbs up from many young guys, "Way to go" from folks, gay and straight, and lots of people telling us how many years they'd been together, too. One baby-boomer woman smiled at us, put her hand over her heart and said "you make me proud to be a woman." Wow. Didn't expect that.

But it was the young gals, gay and straight, who had us crying from laughter. They'd read the sign, then look at us and emit a loud and plaintive "Awwww," like a sound you'd make when seeing a puppy. "Awwww, aren't these old lesbians cute…"

Conservatively, at least 300 cell phones snapped our photo and many a contingent of teens and twenty-somethings crowded in to have their pictures taken with us. We felt like rock stars. Old rock stars. The diversity of the crowd was staggering, often impossible to tell gay from straight. The clothing, demeanor, and signage ranged from wacky to conservative to spectacular.

At one point, a reporter asked if we'd rallied for our rights before this and we recounted tales of the '79, '87, '93, and 2000 marches, also discussing our predecessor Barbara Gittings marching at the White House in the 1960s. "She and her fellow protestors were dressed to the nines," I said, telling the reporter that they had required the men to wear suits and ties and the women to wear dresses and high heels. "I love that!" hollered a guy sporting bright purple hair and so many earrings you could strain linguini through his lobes.

Two women approached us, holding their sign also proclaiming 31 years, though not on this specific day. Our conversation, overheard by a reporter from the *Huffington Post*, turned into a full-fledged interview of the four women she called "the 31 Ones."

Per protocol, each reporter had to ask us our names and ages. As I repeated that big numeral over and over I was pleased by the number of times people responded with "Well, you don't look it." By hour four of standing and holding the sign aloft, I felt it and then some.

When the oral arguments inside the court ended, the plaintiff, Edie Windsor, and her legal team came down the steps to thundering cheers from the crowd. We milled about a few moments more, then packed in our fifteen minutes of fame and headed back to the hotel.

With aching legs, horribly stiff necks from staring in just one direction at each other across the sign all day (how stupid of us not to trade places after a while!), and rotator cuffs throbbing from raising our banner, we collapsed on the hotel bed and turned on the TV.

We made CSPAN, WRC-TV in Washington, a montage of photos on CBS, a mention on Public Television and more. By 4:30 the *Huffington Post* article was posted. My cell phone lit up with texts, messages and calls from friends recounting the places they'd seen our brief celebrity.

By Thursday morning of course, we were, quite literally, yesterday's news.

But what a hoot it was. And now, all we can do is hope that the Supremes heard our message and declare the offensive Defense of Marriage Act unconstitutional. Enough already. I want to retire from the protest business. Equality Now!▼

Overheard at Legislative Hall in Dover: "I don't get this marriage thing. We just gave them civil unions."

THEM? What am I a space alien? A creature from the Rehoboth lagoon? An undocumented worker from Mars? It's humiliating to be described as "them."

And just like all of the minority groups who have come before us and who will surely come after us, I'm sick of having neighbors think of us as THEM. OTHER. LESS THAN. UNEQUAL. SECOND CLASS.

I'm passionately, angrily, tiredly but hopefully done being THEM.

By the time you read this, lots of LGBT folks in Rehoboth and the surrounding communities will have traveled to Dover once again, this time before a state Senate committee, to plead for the right to be treated equally under Delaware law.

And to answer that snooty, attitudinal, bigoted woman at the State House, I say this, "While you grudgingly gave us civil unions, we were happy for that step. It truly did make us financially equal to married couples in Delaware, but it did not go far enough."

Here is how I had the privilege of testifying and describing the situation to the Delaware House of Representatives in Dover a few weeks ago:

"My partner and I have been together over 31 years. As young women, we bought a house, paid taxes, welcomed pets to our family, encouraged each other in our careers, spoiled our nieces and nephews, socialized with neighbors, managed our parents' health crises, turned middle aged, buried our first dog and cat, relocated to Delaware, weathered our own health crises, saved for retirement, said farewell to parents who saw us as married, adopted two new dogs, volunteered in our community, and just now became Medicare eligible—all of this,

together.

We married first in Canada, when marriage equality there became legal. We married again last year, with a big fat Jewish Wedding, recognized as marriage by our religious institution, but only as a civil union in Delaware. So neither ceremony gave us what we need most—a legally recognized marriage equal to our heterosexually married neighbors.

Now, we're retirees and sadly, just lost our remaining 15-year old Schnauzer. The dogs have been a benchmark for our 31 years. We urge the state to end our long run as lesser citizens with a second class term for our relationship. We need Delaware to pass the marriage equality bill so when the Defense of Marriage Act falls, whenever that may be, we will have the one thing we need, a legal marriage, to qualify for Federal equal rights and benefits.

At the moment we're debating whether we're too old for a puppy. Our run with unequal rights has gone on long enough. Please be on the right side of history, and grant all Delaware citizens marriage equality. And we'll let you know what we decide about the puppy. Thank you."

Yes, I got a laugh on the line about the puppy. But it's all too true and too important to be a laughing matter anymore. Frankly, the idea of equality was so foreign to us in the 1970s and 80s as we marched for visibility and protection from discrimination. Sure, we had a hell of a lot of laughs at those grand events. "We're here, we're queer, get used to it" we chanted. We had our dykes on bikes, our brave drag queens, our military heroes coming out.

So too, was it exuberant, joyous and important to march in 1990's Pride parades and fight for the right of gay people to serve in the military. Skirmishing for small victories and safe communities was always fun because we came together as a fun-loving, determined community working to build a bridge to the majority; to **C**reate **A M**ore **P**ositive Rehoboth (the CAMP acronym) and also a more positive world.

But I woke up today, *Letters* deadline looming and realized that for all the marching, advocacy, fund-raising, letter writing, speech-giving and emotional investment, to lots of Delawareans we are still THEM.

The vote for full marriage equality in the Delaware House was victorious. Our House of Delegates, led by Speaker of the House Pete Schwartzkopf voted in favor of marriage equality. It was a historic and delicious victory.

But now the vote goes to the Senate, which is not a sure thing. We need 11 YES votes in the Senate. And the difference between full marriage equality and the painful continuation of unequal status for those some call THEM could rest on the senator from our own Sussex County district. This senator has the privilege of representing LGBT constituents in literally hundreds of same-sex households. Will he vote for our equality or to keep us as second class citizens? Will we stay in the THEM column? It may just be up to our own state senator.

Frankly, these THEM are sick of living in sin. We want to be declared legally wed in Delaware. That's a much better environment in which to raise a puppy. ▼

May 2013

For me, it was the gavel heard 'round my world.

As I write this, I am still not certain exactly how to describe the events and emotions of Tuesday, May 7, at Legislative Hall in Dover, Delaware. That was the almost-unbelievable day when the Marriage Equality Bill, HB 75, already passed in the Delaware House of Representatives, passed in the Delaware Senate, making same-gender marriage the law in Delaware.

Yes, it's state law, not yet federal, but I never thought I'd see even this much in my lifetime, and I am still giddy from the wonderful shock.

On the day of the vote I was in Senator Karen Peterson's small office at Legislative Hall listening to the proceedings on a squawk box. I'd arrived from teaching a class too late to get a gallery seat. Equality Delaware President Lisa Goodman spied me loitering in the lobby and escorted me to the senator's office. There, I joined several Equality Delaware volunteers and Stonewall Democrats as Lisa rushed back to the Senate floor, where she, attorney Mark Purpura, and Senator David Sokola, among others, started the day's business of making history.

For three long hours I sat in the senator's office, listening to the encouraging testimony of marriage equality proponents alternating with the disheartening, infuriating, and often ignorant testimony of the "No Genderless Marriage" team. I squirmed in my chair, listening to their irrational fears and mostly irrelevant arguments, nervous about the upcoming vote and seemingly struck by restless body syndrome. Would all the senators who'd promised YES votes show up? We needed 11 YEAs from the 21 senators. What was about to happen? I fidgeted and fidgeted some more.

While Dixiecrat Democratic Senator Venables droned on about the perils of gay marriage, we learned one of the promised YEAs was missing. "Find him!" came a cry in the hallway, a fellow senator rushing to action.

Bible verse after Bible verse came over the speaker as angry, fearful people testified to their worry that children would be taught gay marriage is, gasp, normal! And what about florists who don't want to provide arrangements for gay weddings? Or photographers who don't want to snap pix of gay people?

Senators and Equality Delaware lawyers happily let everyone know that since 2009 there has been a law on the books forbidding discrimination against gay people by the likes of florists, photographers, and any other business accommodating the public. And guess what? There's been hardly a complaint or a problem since. Another irrational argument trounced.

By this time the missing YES voter was in the chamber and warm, rational words continued to alternate with demeaning, hurtful and just plain stupid ones.

An amazing exchange occurred when Senator Peterson herself answered a question that was both foolish and denigrating to gay people. In a surprise moment, the senator flung open her own closet door in an emotional speech about her 24-year relationship with her partner, saying, "Neither I nor my partner chose to be gay any more than heterosexuals chose to be straight. If my happiness somehow demeans or diminishes your marriage then you need to work on your marriage." It was a jaw-dropping, applause-invoking moment in the chamber and an eye-popping, "Did she just come out???" moment right there in Senator Karen Peterson's office.

When the seemingly endless ugly testimony finally stopped, I could feel tension wash over the room as if one of our famous coastal fogs had just rolled in. A young Equality Delaware staffer leaned on Senator Peterson's desk and, as the roll was called, checked off names with Yea or Nay. Along the way, we had a surprise YES from Senator Bethany Hall-Long of Middletown, and by vote's end there were 12 in favor, 9 against.

When the Senate president announced the passage of HB75 there was a stunned silence and a collective intake of breath as our small group then broke into cheers and applause. One second later, the din delayed by distance, we heard the thunderous cheers, whoops and hollers from the Senate chamber and gallery.

"We're all supposed to go to the Governor's office," announced the young staffer. "He's going to sign the bill right now."

Because of where we had been holed up, we hit the grand staircase in the building before most people and practically ran up to the Governor's office. My knees were jelly, and elated butterflies danced in my stomach. This was really happening! In Delaware!

Bonnie and I had just arrived at the outer office door when a grinning Governor Jack Markell came through it—and we were among the first people the governor hugged and congratulated.

It brought me right back to years ago when then-state comptroller Markell spoke up early and often, at his own political peril, for our cause; when Speaker Schwartzkopf first ran for election as an underdog in our district and he bravely made the decision to fight aggressively for our rights; to when Steve and Murray first started CAMP Rehoboth, fighting for simple safety and respect for LGBT residents. Look how far we've come thanks to all our political allies, tireless activists and incessant advocates.

For me, it was a stunning moment, and thrilling as this transplanted New Yorker realized she lived in such a small state that the governor was able to call out "Fay! Bonnie! Congratulations!"

With more than 200 marriage equality supporters standing on the grand staircase and around the balcony on the second floor, we heard a smiling Governor Markell tell us, "I do not intend to make any of you wait one moment longer. Delaware should be, is and will be a welcoming place to live and love and to raise a family for all who call our great state home."

I stood with my wife on the state house staircase and knew that Delaware considered our marriage truly equal to all others.

And with that, a small table was placed on the staircase landing so the governor could stand amid many of the senators who voted yes, the activists from Equality Delaware, and other marriage equality supporters and sign the bill that had passed only a few minutes before.

I'm still having trouble believing it. As you know, I've always adored my hometown of Rehoboth Beach for its embrace of its gay residents and visitors. But now the whole state, tiny as it may be, is onboard with our civil rights. Pretty darn amazing. ▼

May 2013

IT'S TIME FOR THE NEXT CHAPTER

Well, the rumors are flying!

Friends here in town and even down south have been peppered with calls. "Are Fay and Bonnie moving?" "Are they running away in the RV?" "Are they going to live at Jellystone Park with Yogi Bear?" I guess they saw the FOR SALE sign on our weed-riddled lawn.

NO!!! We are NOT leaving Rehoboth. That would break our hearts. But the rumor mill has been churning ever since we began a hunt for the perfect retirement dwelling. You know what they say in this town—don't worry if you don't know what you're doing, someone else will. Or guess, fabricate, or surmise. So here's the real story.

Where once we (the Royal WE) enjoyed gunning our pet riding mower over turf on the homestead, we no longer feel the thrill. We do feel the sciatica. We are sick of paying to open and close the watering system, when we could be using those funds at our favorite watering hole. Personally, we resent spending our martini money on mulch.

So recently, we woke up, smelled the Starbucks, and saw the forest for the trees. Trees, I might add, we lovingly planted in 1999 when this place was the little house on the prairie. By this time they're a threat to the roof. So after 14 years of mulching, pruning, watering, feeding, and otherwise giving aid and comfort to the greenery, I had to kill them. It was enough to make me want to chug Round-Up.

And we got sick of spending the equivalent of several gourmet dinners just to recoat the driveway every year. Likewise money spent on crawl space ventilation and weed whacker string. Uncle!!! So it's time to put yard work and exterior maintenance out to somebody else's pasture. We're going to downsize, or as the PR flaks say, "rightsize." We have whacked our last weed.

It's been 18 years since we first docked in Dewey in our floating home. News of our arrival was detailed in the pages of *Letters from CAMP Rehoboth*, and every move we've made since then has been documented there as well. From the boat to a condo, then a second condo and finally to our house in the "suburbs" of Rehoboth. Then came the RV as an additional guest cottage.

So it's time for the next chapter. For a brief shining moment we considered coming full circle, renting a slip in Dewey and living aboard a boat again. But we came to our senses. Leaping on and off a rocking boat on a windy night was a challenge when we were in our forties, but now we'd have to line the dock with granny grab bars and still risk an occasional cold bath. Besides, the gentle roll of the boat that used to lull us to sleep, will now just exacerbate the reflux. The final nail in the gangplank was picturing 3 a.m. pee breaks, perched on a moving target. No thanks.

Okay, so where could we live, keep the trappings and privacy of a single family home but avoid mowing and mulching? After much mulling and financial planning, we decided to sell our house and buy a manufactured home. A linear estate. A mobile home that stays put. Once we sell our house, we will be moving to a beautiful mobile resort community, still here in Rehoboth Beach.

Oh, I know the jokes. You might be trailer trash if: the Salvation Army declines your furniture; you offer to give someone the shirt off your back and they don't want it; you have the local taxidermist on speed dial; you come back from the dump with more than you took; or you have a complete set of salad bowls and they all say "Cool Whip" on the side.

Well, the truth is, you may be ripe for a manufactured home if you want a place where your annual tax bill is lower than dinner for two (seriously); your house is registered at the DMV (honest); there are gorgeous cherry trees and pretty land-scaping all over and you don't have to mow it, mulch it or feed it; you have a pool and exercise room without needing a gym membership; and finally, you can lock the door and travel without a care in the world.

So that's the plan. Our new home will be Base Camp Rehoboth so we can enjoy the beautiful months here at home and travel in the RV when there's ice and snow on the boardwalk.

Not that the transition will be easy. The new place is tiny. The office where columns like this will be written is so small (how small is it?) you need to go out in the hall to change your mind; you put a key in the door lock and break a window; you trade your desktop computer for a laptop. And for that matter, does anybody reading this want a gorgeous roll top desk? It won't fit through the door.

So the task before us, unlike the new house, is huge. We have to downsize; de-accessorize and pick our way through 14 years of accumulated possessions. How did we collect all this? The Mother of All Yard Sales (Part I) will be next week on our driveway. By then we will have made painful decisions about what to keep and what to let go.

The next great adventure begins. In the meantime, you might be manufactured home material if you want a house where you can party on and let the good times roll without using all your disposable income for yard waste bags shredded mulch. I'm ready. ▼

June 2013

About the only thing associated with walking I haven't done lately is taken a long walk off a short pier. But, I suspect I'll get to that come August.

In a completely uncharacteristic move, I have taken up walking for health. I walk between one and two miles a day and oddly enough, I like it. Since January I haven't missed a day.

Now that also might have something to do with my diet and exercise-obsessed best friend who will verbally eviscerate me if I skip a day. But frankly, scary as that prospect is, and as oxymoronic as this may sound, I enjoy the exercise.

Not that it's been easy. At first, I dutifully schlepped along with my mile mentor and got pains in my shins, medically known as shin splits. That's positively the only thing I have ever had in common with a ballerina. Trust me.

Then I had to build up my stamina. For a person who got winded walking to the mail box, this was a chore. Initially, I only had enough air to either walk or talk, not both. Consequently, I schlepped along quietly, which frightened the drill sergeant beside me. Me not talking is like me not breathing. But luckily, I soon built up to walking and grumbling at the same time. Much better. Walking and chewing gum was still in the future.

"It's time you got a pedometer," announced my relentless self-appointed guru.

"Why?"

"So you can know exactly how many tenths of a mile you've been complaining."

Okay, so I bought the pedometer. The directions said I could attach it to my belt, pocket or shoe laces. Shoe laces seemed easy.

Days went by and I consistently got credit for far more miles than I walked. What the heck? It wasn't until I was watching television one night and looked down to realize that a shoe is really not the proper place for a pedometer if you have restless leg syndrome. I was eating popcorn and watching *Mad Men* and the pedometer thought I was doing a 5K.

A person's weight and the distance you walk determine the calories you burn from walking. A rule of thumb is 100 calories burned per mile for somebody my weight. But all I have to do is eat a cookie the size of my thumb and there goes the benefit. For last week's dinner at Rehoboth's famed Blue Moon Restaurant penance is an extra 27 miles.

So obviously, watching your calories goes hand in hand with walking for weight loss. I've been watching my calories for years—watching them go directly into my mouth without actually bothering to count them. Now, I'm a little more attentive. While it's hard to crave a Hershey Bar when you know you have to walk to Virginia to burn it off, sadly I can still do it.

Since my walk on the wild side began, I have strolled two miles on a Florida beach, twenty blocks at a time in Manhattan, and frequently the two miles up and back on the Rehoboth Boardwalk. I try to walk early in the morning, before the Funnel Cake place has time to open.

Once, doing my mile on a trip to Maryland, I came to understand how lucky we are not to have a measurable hill in all of Delaware. The same distance I breeze through at home is like climbing Kilimanjaro there. A Sherpa with oxygen tanks and Gatorade would have helped.

On most days I take an iPod along but I have to be careful. Anything with a disco beat has me walking and pointing like John Travolta in *Saturday Night Fever*. Persons not hearing the music see this and think I have imaginary cooties. Show tunes are even worse. It's amazing how frightened people can become seeing somebody exhibiting Ethel Merman body language. Listening to *Cats* could get me picked up by animal control.

Actually, one day last spring it was a very good thing I was in fighting trim for a walk. I was near the boardwalk enjoying a martini (96 calories) when it started to rain. Then pour. Then deluge. I had to be at the Convention Center in twenty minutes and, having no raincoat or umbrella, my only choice seemed like arriving wet and wild and not in a good way.

With no let-up in sight, I found a large plastic trash bag, cut neck and arm holes and slipped it on like a mu-mu. A pal grabbed another bag for my head, wrapping me in a Gloria Swanson, *Sunset Boulevard* turban. I gulped the rest of my vodka and headed out.

Turbaned and ziplocked, a veritable Glad bag lady, I marched down the street, ignoring mobs of rain-coated tourists staring and laughing. Thanks to my daily walking regimen, my trip in Hefty Bag chic took less time than it might have, eliminating humiliation exposure. I arrived high *and* dry.

So this walking thing has its benefits. I'm losing weight, listening to more music and breathing easier. Now that I've made deadline with this article, I'm off to walk. Besides, Cruela the Walker will be calling any minute to see how I've done today. I can't wait to tell her I've learned to walk and chew gum. Progress. ▼

June 2013

THE TONY AWARDS, UP CLOSE AND PERSONAL

"Cast to your opening positions."

The booming voice comes over the sound system at 9:55 a.m. I'm sitting halfway back in the orchestra—which, considering this is the enormous art deco cavern that is Radio City Music Hall, is a considerable distance from the stage.

Around me hover TV cameras, boom operators, sound engineers, and a two-story revolving crane hoisting a camera to catch celebrities in their seats and winners coming down the aisles. This is dress rehearsal for the 67th Annual Tony Awards, and I'm fascinated by every single thing happening around me.

I last went to the Tony Awards in 1971 for the 25th Anniversary of the Tonys. I was just out of college, having scored tickets with a friend. Apparently, it hadn't been a banner year on Broadway because the entire show featured classic performances from the recent Golden Era of musicals. I saw Yul Brynner do a scene from *The King and I*, Carol Channing sing from *Hello, Dolly!*, and the highlight for me, Angela Lansbury and Bea Arthur reprise "Bosom Buddies" from *Mame*.

Now it's more than 40 years later, and thanks to a friend who knows the producer, I'm back at the Tonys. Well, the dress rehearsal, which, I know will be even more interesting than the real thing.

"We will be using all effects, all elevators, everything. This is dress rehearsal. 45 seconds...stand by..."

And there's Neil Patrick Harris, launching into one of the most spectacular opening numbers ever, complete with circus performers from *Pippin*, newspaper boys from *Newsies*, orphans from *Annie*, and great big, glorious drag queens from *Kinky Boots*. There are lyrics about Billy Porter's ass, drag queens, and Broadway being swarmed by child actors, proving once again, that the Tonys are indeed the gay Super Bowl. Neil Patrick Harris' opening number last year was "The Tonys—not just for gays anymore!" but frankly who are we kidding? The show is gay, gay, gay.

All of the nominees and celebrity ticket-holders are still in bed on this Sunday morning in New York, while stand-ins hold their assigned seats so cameras can practice pick-ups. Stand-in actors also play presenters, filling in for the likes of Tom Hanks and Cuba Gooding, Jr.

"And the winner is—FOR THIS REHEARSAL ONLY..."

The stand-ins announce random names, and give phony speeches, thanking their mothers, agents, and lovers, some pausing to make a case to the audience for going to Broadway shows early and often. One handsome actor, standing in for a phony *Kinky Boots* winner (although I sit here hoping *Kinky Boots* will take it tonight) said, "I'd like to have one of those cute *Newsie* boys to take home."

We all laugh. By all, I mean me and Bonnie and the hundred or so gay men sprinkled throughout the orchestra. There are a smattering of straight couples, obviously in the business, and a few hapless much-older straight men on the arms of well-dressed women who have had lots of "work done." But seriously, the crowd is overwhelmingly, fantastically gay.

After suffering though a big number from the musical *Matilda*, which by the way I hated, although the critics raved, I get to see Jane Lynch gleefully belt out a number from *Annie*. The big musical number from *Pippin* shows that the 1970s musical has been re-imagined with acrobats, magic acts, and jugglers. *Pippin du Soleil*.

Jessie Tyler Ferguson shows up to rehearse his lines, asking for the correct pronunciation of one of the nominee's names. "Glad I came to rehearse," he says.

Actually, as the hour gets later, more celebrities show up to try out their presenter speeches, including some casually dressed pros—Sally Field, Patti LuPone, Bernadette Peters, Matthew Morrison, and more. Even the dog from *Annie* makes an appearance, providing our emcee with a face full of dog slobber.

The show proceeds in real time, with breaks for commercials where techies scramble to get the scenery ready for the big musical numbers. One or two set pieces slide on stage, but the backgrounds are projections. Clever!

"Back in five seconds, can we have some applause please?" We obey.

The boom camera sweeps the gigantic theatre like a graceful giraffe, the base of its neck sporting weights to keep it grounded. Uh-Oh, there's a glitch! The curtain isn't in place.

"Did you wake up this morning and wonder why we have a dress rehearsal? This is why," quips Neil Patrick Harris. A hundred stagehands come running and fussing and rigging.

Then comes the most moving part of the rehearsal. The words "In Memoriam" appear on an upstage screen and Cyndi Lauper and her band file on to do a sweet rendition of "True Colors" with photos and names appearing behind them.

Cyndi's up for a Tony for best music and lyrics for *Kinky Boots*. I imagine she's nervous. But, her performance is poignant and perfect.

Two last "winners" for this rehearsal only come up on stage, mumble their faux appreciation and the sparkling emcee says, "That's it folks!!! Goodnight."

What? No closing number??? Guess not. And out we go.

By 6:30 p.m., after a late lunch at Carnegie Deli, a walk through the Village, and checking in at the Chelsea Pines Inn, we go to the owner's suite at the hotel, where we've been invited to watch the Tonys. The hotel owner, if you have not heard this story, is my former high school prom date, now the proprietor of the number two B&B in NYC, according to Trip Advisor. The hotel is gorgeous, his apartment there, magnificent. And he's still as adorable as ever, I might add.

From the ceiling comes a huge movie screen projecting the CBS annual *Tony Awards* presentation. There's the opening number, compete with close-ups, brought to life by those big boom cameras.

Nathan Lane, David Hyde Pierce, and Harvey Fierstein sit where their doubles had been; Cuba Gooding, Jr., stumbles over the names of the nominees because he slept in this morning; smooth, professional readings rise from Patti LuPone and Sally Field; Tom Hanks smiles from his seat, held that morning by an exuberant older woman; everything goes like clockwork.

Jokes which fell flat this morning are gone; a couple of awkward presenter's comments are MIA, and damn, if that dog from *Annie* didn't slobber on cue again for the real show.

And this time the awards are not for this rehearsal only. *Kinky Boots* dominates with six Awards, including Cyndi Lauper for her words and music; *Matilda* doesn't win for Best Musical (Yay!) and *Kinky Boots* does. Cecily Tyson is crowned Best Actress; the cast of *Who's Afraid of Virginia Wolfe* does well, and *Pippin* shines in the revival category.

But wait! There IS a closing number. Neil Patrick Harris manages to sing enormously clever lyrics about all the winners! They must have written the number featuring every single possibility, frantically crossing out non-winners from the wings. That really IS show business! It was a tongue-twisting triumph of a closing number, adding to the glorious production. I loved every single minute.

I think I'll wait less than 40 years to go back. ▼

June 2013

It Took the Entire 65 Years of My Life to Get Here

"You have until 4 o'clock to do a new column. Probably not enough time," editor Steve Elkins said.

Not enough time to make this deadline after waiting 65 years to be a full citizen of the United States? Watch me.

Today, Wednesday, June 26, at about 10 a.m., DOMA (the ill-conceived Bill Clinton law banning federal recognition of gay marriage in the U.S.) was overturned by a mostly-conservative U.S. Supreme Court. I watched, spell-bound, in my living room as commentator Rachel Maddow, former Congressman Barney Frank and a parade of others described how this (apparently) straight but apparently not narrow (at least five judges, anyway) court struck down DOMA as unconstitutional and granted full marriage rights to same sex couples in states where gay marriage is legal.

I never thought I'd see this in my lifetime. In fact, for the first 45 years of my lifetime I never even conceived of it. In the beginning, the very word "gay" made me sick. Was I one? And if so, based on furtive, whispered comments and society's fear I was certain I'd have an unhappy, miserable life.

I never thought I'd see this day when I was hiding in the closet through high school and college; when homosexual conduct itself was still illegal; when I was guiltily sneaking around bad neighborhoods and seedy bars to meet others like myself; when I was ashamed and terrified to be outed at work.

Could I see this day coming when I sweated bullets about admitting I was gay to my parents? Did I think this possible when Bonnie couldn't use her VA benefit to buy a house because we weren't married? When doctors dismissed me as a mere "friend" when Bonnie was in the hospital? When I had to pay thousands and thousands of dollars extra for my own catastrophic individual health insurance because I wasn't considered a spouse by Bonnie's employer?

I never pictured this happening when I started writing for the *Washington Blade* (under a pen name so I would not lose my job) in the 1980s; when I marched on Washington in '87, '93, and 2000; when I began writing for *Letters* (under my |own byline) in 1996; as I wrote columns about protecting our relationships with the proper paperwork, railing against discrimination for AIDS patients, attacking conservative politicians as they attacked and denigrated us.

But in the last ten years, as gay marriage became more and more of a possibility in Bright Blue states, I still never dreamed our federal government would recognize me and my wife (married in Canada in 2003) as full married citizens.

I never dreamed this would happen as I went to Dover to support CAMP Rehoboth and Equality Delaware in their successful fight for gay marriage in Delaware; when our amazing Speaker of the House Pete Schwartzkopf led the charge for anti-discrimination and equality; when our legislators did the right and just thing; when Equality Delaware's Lisa Goodman and Mark Purpura engineered the words and spirit behind this momentous action. And when our amazingly supportive Governor Jack Markell instantly signed the bill so "you won't have to wait one minute longer!"

But today? This conservative court striking down DOMA? This is the big one. I am recognized as a full, proud citizen by the U.S. government. The hell with what Justice Scalia, the Family Research Council and millions of ignorant or bigoted people think. Today, in Delaware, as it relates to the federal government, we have achieved marriage equality.

You know, when I was about eight years old, I was flipping through a copy of *The New Yorker* on my parents' coffee table, looking at the cartoons. Most of them I didn't understand. But one drawing wasn't a cartoon really, but an illustration with a story. It showed an African American man, slouched down, driving a horse-drawn wagon. In the second panel of the drawing, the wagon passed the Mason-Dixon line into the Northern part of the country. The wagon driver was proudly sitting up, head held high.

My mother, with her ever-present progressive and liberal views, explained the drawing to me. I got it.

But I get it so much more today. Damn. It really does get better. ▼

June 2013

We knew this was the year to be at the New York City Gay Pride Parade. Let's face it, with the DOMA ruling having come down days before, and Edie Windsor set to be parade Grand Marshal, we had lots to celebrate.

As soon as we hit Manhattan we knew it was going to be something special. Rainbow flags flew everywhere, even in the most unlikely places, like corner falafel trucks. Entire buildings had been draped in rainbow colors, as banks, and drugs stores and retailers all celebrated with the LGBT community. Pretty amazing, actually.

After a weekend of wine, women, and song we lined up Sunday morning for the parade at 33rd Street and 5th Avenue, the starting point. Once launched, the parade would wind downtown for hours to the Village and Christopher Street where the night would be capped with celebrations, street gatherings, and ultimately fireworks over the river at 11 p.m. Pretty good public celebration for a community still considered criminal in the 60s. Makes ya think, doesn't it?

We'd gotten there early enough to be in the front, along the police barricades, for a perfect view of our heroine Edie Windsor when she passed by. With the sun beating down and huge crowds jockeying for position, it was hot and a hoot. Spectators seemed made up of equal parts gays, straights, tourists, children, and pets. Vendors sold rainbow flags, rainbow roses, rainbow crap of all kinds.

Does anybody remember Rollerena? In the 70s, this tall, thin drag queen used to roller skate around Manhattan, always making a festive appearance at pride parades. We found ourselves standing next to this disco-era celebrity by the barricades. She may have given up her skates, but she still looked like a million bucks as she and her gaudily dressed friends waited to step into the parade as it passed by.

First we heard motorcycles revving—ah, the dykes on bikes, love them! Gone are the days when they'd lead the parade in pants and vests, breasts flapping in the wind. This posse was fully dressed, cheering us as we cheered them, and heady with celebration.

And then we heard it. Whoops and hollers and cheers spreading toward us like a stadium wave, as the convertible with Edie Windsor came into view. Slowly the car rolled down the block, Ms. Windsor, all in white, draped in a rainbow sash, wide-brimmed hat on her head, smiling, waving, standing up to greet the community. People screamed and waved. Men bowed in reverence, drag queens squealed. And as this victorious plaintiff moved along, thousands of people blew Dinah Shore "mwah!" kisses in her direction. I will never forget the moment.

Next came all kinds of corporate sponsors, their employees marching along, tossing products to the crowd: rainbow lip gloss, packets of sunscreen, key chains, vitamin water, the works. Between the banks, airlines, and phone companies, it was hard to believe it was a gay pride parade, not the Macy's Thanksgiving Day Parade. Although make no mistake. We were giving thanks to Edie and the Supremes.

And pretty soon, the LGBT organizations, bars, and businesses, with their fancy floats, disco beats, and scantily clad revelers rolled by, reminding us just what kind of happy parade this was. After about an hour schvitzing in the hot sun, we moved along, walking uptown, and taking in a whole city bathed in gay pride.

We spent the rest of the day uptown, dining with friends and shaking our heads in wonder at the sea of rainbow decorations, festive LGBT folks clogging the streets, and a feeling of victory, freedom, and renewed patriotism as we faced the July 4th weekend.

By evening, we hopped a cab back downtown, as I felt the need to be at the Stonewall Inn on this historic night. Yeah, me and 100,000 other people. The cab got mired in traffic six blocks away so we bailed and trudged through the masses, getting glitter-bombed en route. Standing on the street in front of the Stonewall had to suffice, as it was packed and hemorrhaging pierced, tattooed, young people, of every ethnicity, and mode of dress. Or undress. Everyone's mood identical—unfettered joy.

At that point, my previously imbibed Cosmos caught up with me. Crisis. I had to pee. Bonnie and I fought our way through the crush of bodies, almost all of them 30 to omigod 40 years younger than we, and across the street to a Starbucks. Inside, a long bathroom line formed with an employee checking receipts to make certain only customers used the facilities.

I cast no blame. Made perfect sense given the teeming humanity outside. But I hadda pee! Me, to the 18-year old employee: "I swear I will buy an iced coffee after I pee, but this is an old-lady emergency. Please take pity on us."

He did, and let us pre-pee. We bought iced decaf and headed out through the madness and back uptown. Of course, I never thought I'd see federal recognition of gay marriage in my lifetime; never thought I'd see all of New York City celebrating the rainbow nation; never thought I'd be able to walk from Christopher Street through the throngs to the hotel at 14th Street. But we did, with fireworks exploding in the sky behind us. With every blast we turned to watch, grinning and then walking on air up the street, shedding glitter and glee with every step. We're queer, we're still here, jeez, they got used to it.▼

July 2013

TESTING WHETHER THIS NATION,
OR ANY NATION CAN LONG ENDURE

If you think summer traffic at the beach is bad, think again. Yes, I know. It often seems you can gestate a baby in the time it takes to creep down Route One to Rehoboth Avenue, but it's nothing compared to my recent Battle of Bull Run on Route 66 in Virginia.

The world will little note, nor long remember what I say here, but oy, it was a mess! I went to visit an ailing friend one day, leaving Rehoboth at 3 p.m. on a Thursday, heading for that cradle of Civil War history, Manassas, VA. It was remarkably clear sailing to the Bay Bridge, then DC, oddly traffic-free through the Nation's Capital, despite it being 5:30 p.m. on a work day.

Then, picture this. Aggravation strikes in a caravan of brake lights at the start of Route 66 in Arlington. With 18 miles to go, I'm now rolling at between two and four mph, timed perfectly to arrive for tomorrow's breakfast. Robert E. Lee's whole Bull Run campaign didn't take this long.

It's agonizingly slow, but even the high occupancy lanes are wretchedly inert. Hah! Many drivers, determined to qualify for the HOV lane, pick up commuting strangers. It's bad enough cursing to myself in the car, but imagine enduring this motionless migration with a stranger making small talk. Torture!

Oh good, the guy behind me thinks honking for thirty seconds over Fairfax helps. Flipping him the bird is counter-productive; we'll be joined at the bumper for the rest of the war.

Now we're inching past the Virginia Firearms Museum. Can I get a gun and shoot myself? Likewise, the Manassas Antique show is touted on a billboard. My late model car will be ready for it when I arrive there. Splat, splat, splat, big floppy raindrops plummet, wipers scratching the windshield like fingernails on a blackboard. Brake lights flash on and off like some code from aliens. Indeed, there is a close encounter of the fender kind one lane over. As we creep on, I picture Union soldiers with muskets, crawling on their bellies faster than this.

Close to two hours later I arrive at my destination in a sweaty frazzle, only to discover my friend, supposedly home from the hospital, is actually stranded in her daughter's over-heating car at one of the Route 66 exits.

"Jump in my car, we'll go rescue them," says her husband, "I'll take the overheating car to a garage and you can drive her home in this one."

Back into battle? He's got to be kidding.

Sadly, no. We fight the second Battle of Bull Run, from Manassas back to Fairfax, literally crossing, once again, that winding waterway that ran red during the Civil War. We, mean-while, see red as traffic still hasn't lessened, taking us another 80 minutes to go 14 miles. I think I saw Stonewall Jackson in the Subaru next to me.

We make it to Chantilly only to swap cars and passengers and reverse course. Even the War Between the States didn't have a third Bull Run battle.

It gets worse. Now I'm trapped in the back seat with a three and five year old who are behaving no better than most of the commuters imprisoned on Route 66. Among this confederacy of dunces, the kids throw shoes at mom and grandmom in the front seat, squeal, spit, hit each other and me, and I wonder if violence like this has broken out between those HOV drivers and their babbling strangers.

An excruciating hour passes, but we finally arrive back at my friend's home for the all-important two-hour visit. Her physical health is improved; my mental health, not so much. To avoid further angst, I choose not to get my kicks on Route 66 come morning but instead, head back to DC that night.

Holy Jefferson Davis, now there's road construction! If anything, the pace is even slower than the misnamed descriptor "rush hour" and more frustrating for its surprise.

Blinding work lights and a parade of traffic cones accompany the misery of retracing my steps along these Civil War battlefields. Margaret Mitchell didn't take this long to write *Gone With The Wind*.

I find a place to stay en route and in the morning calculate my escape to coincide with abated traffic.

Come the morning after, cruising at the speed limit, Bay Bridge bound in the rain, traffic suddenly halts near Annapolis. Too late to be the morning crush and too early for beach traffic, what the Robert E. Lee is this? Then, the rain becomes more of a thundering monsoon. Visibility drops to nothing, the bridge is enveloped in a hundred-year fog and fender benders ensue.

This gives rise to Maryland's take on brother against brother as uncivil war erupts. Drivers swerve on my left flank, cut each other off, jockey to get through Easy Pass and the bridge. Four freakin' miles take over an hour. I should be shot for having had the Starbucks Double-Shot coffee. My bladder is screaming as I search the front and back seats for a potential open container should the need arise. I clench my teeth and everything else. Inching along, I must now cede my position to the battalion behind me as I skulk off road to find a potty. Relief and an Egg McMuffin later, I am back in the crawling caravan.

Talk radio incites me. Music of the 80s makes me gag. Listening to the garbled AM radio announcement from the department of transportation is no help at all. I choose silence with the occasional honk and epithet.

Twelve miles takes two and a half more hours. Auuggghhh!!!!

By the time I get home to Delaware, the South could have risen again, So, too, my blood pressure. The trip back took five and a half hours before I was freed from my automobile. Yes, I emit a "Woo-Hoo!" as my (*here it comes*) emancipation proclamation.

For my trip to Virginia I sat in excruciating traffic for a full dozen of the twenty-six hours I was gone. It didn't take Abraham Lincoln that long to ride in a horse and buggy from Washington to Gettysburg to deliver his Address.

Is Route One at its worst a piece of cake? You bet your sweet asphalt. This driver staying local is a more perfect union.▼

July 2013

Okay, first things first, we have to sell our house and its three quarters of an acre. The realtor said "You've got to unclutter this place and make it seem like a model home. All those bright colored walls have to go. The personal pictures, gone! Get rid of everything on the kitchen counter!"

Okay, maybe the place did look a little like Spencer's Gifts after a hurricane, but unclutter completely? We spent the first two weeks of June painting the walls beige. We got our recommended 10,000 steps a day in, much of it up and down ladders. Gone are the flashy colors and walls full of family photos and memorabilia. Missing are the Schnauzer statues and geegaws. All the walls are now Sherman Williams Latte. And trust me, you need a double shot latte just to stay out of a coma in here. And we installed fresh, neutral blah carpet to go with the neutral blah walls.

And clean! You could do an appendectomy on the kitchen counter. And bland! It's like living at the Days Inn, which wouldn't be bad if we had room service. And of course, we've been afraid to put down a glass for fear of making a ring on the coffee table. Listing and showing a home is a special kind of hell.

So we moved into the RV on the driveway. Seriously, it was our only choice.

For one thing, every time the house was shown, we'd leave and shop for things for the new house. Four thousand dollars' worth of appliances later, it had to stop. Secondly, it's hard to actually live in a house on the market. We'd be eating lunch, a realtor would call, and unless we wanted the place to look like we fled one step ahead of the mob, it took a frantic effort to make the place pristine. Living in the RV was just easier.

And "Let there be light!" Real estate etiquette says a home on the market should glow. Every time we exited it was like a bonfire, visible from the space station. You could have a Nats game in there. It was our own personal Motel 6. We'll leave the light on for ya. Also, the electric bill.

Blessedly, by the end of July, we had a contract on the old house and were up to our elbows spackling and painting the new one. We'd downsized by way of a yard sale, unloading Harry Potter CDs, Billy Joel and Beach Boys on vinyl, decades-old furniture ("The 80s called and they want your coffee table back"), the gently used lawn mower and carpet steamer, the queen bed that won't fit in the new guest compartment and much more. A local thrift shop and the dump benefitted from leftovers.

At deadline, as I sit typing in my office devoid of most books and all personality, we still own more assets than will squeeze into our new house. Another sale is pending. Books, posters and albums I held as essential two months ago, now scream "What were you thinking???" Self-help manuals like *Fence and Deck Plans* or *Landscaping Solutions* gotta go. Frankly, I think we chose the perfect landscaping solution. It's somebody else's problem.

I am keeping the book *1000 Places to See Before You Die* and *Fodor's Essential USA*. As I write, we are about to leave for a vacation in the RV (our house on wheels), with plans to move into the new house (technically also a house with wheels, but one with a skirt around the perimeter) in early September.

We have miles to go (both figuratively and literally) before we sleep in the new place. But I am already using the community pool and clubhouse exercise equipment. Both modes of downsizing are going full speed ahead. And I pray we will come through the move two clothing sizes lower with a home that looks less like *Sordid Lives* and more like a sophisticated boutique hotel suite. I shall keep you posted.

In the meantime, if you need a 1970s chrome coffee table, the 1982 version of Trivial Pursuit, a Ouija board, a copy of Khalil Gibran's *The Prophet*, or Streisand on vinyl, you're too late. Downsizing can be painful. ▼

August 2013

Tuesday, July 30

Off to Canada we go! Fought with and cursed the Rand McNally GPS all morning Monday until we stopped in Poughkeepsie to buy a Garmin.

Bonnie, unwilling to give up on her special RV GPS kept it on while we learned to use the Garmin. I didn't know whether I was hearing voices or it was just the competing GPS women. Finally I had to sit on one device to muffle the arguing and there are a lot of jokes I could make here about pulling directions out of my ass, but I will refrain.

After about an hour of this insanity Bonnie hollered "For pity's sake, don't we have a map???" and I went to see if we had one of those antique travel thingies. My mate was not amused when I asked if she wanted the one on parchment or carbon paper.

Drove through the Adirondacks and across the border into Canada, where this time they did not question the amount of liquor we were carrying for personal consumption. I guess they care less about boozehounds in Quebec Province than they did last summer in New Brunswick. Got to the campground by 7 p.m. and grilled steaks on the George Foreman, sipping a 1991 Châteauneuf-du-Pape. I love camping…

This morning we drove to the old port and old city in Montreal. Walked and walked all over this vibrant, gorgeous city, then took a double decker Grey Line tour…this place is full of public art and bicycles, plus galleries, bistros, and shopping, shopping, shopping. We took photos of the stuff we might have bought if we weren't moving to a tiny house.

After sightseeing all day today, we've decided to go on a jet boat through the St. Lawrence River rapids tomorrow. We've heard it's wet but not scary. Hope so. I generally avoid activities that advise you to bring along a change of clothes.

Thursday, August 1

No, we did not drown on the rapids. Just had no internet connection when we got back..

The jet boat was fantastic—huge rapids at high speeds. Like a combination rollercoaster and sinus wash. Drenched and laughing all the way. That we were the oldest people on board both worried and pleased me.

Later we visited Le Village, the gay part of town. "Look at those pink balls!" said Bonnie, something in her tone causing me to respond "Excuuuse me?"

Rounding the corner we saw an avenue with strings of pink plastic balls strung high over the street for blocks and blocks on end. This was clearly the gaycation part of our trip, where we had a great lunch, people watched and loved that the window of the store across the street featured two buff male mannequins wearing only pink speedos. And this was an eyeglass store.

Today we are off to the Museum des Beaux-Arts for a Chihuly glass exhibit.

Saturday, August secondish

Yesterday, in addition to the stunning museum exhibit in Vieux Quebec (Old city), we schlepped up and down miles of ramparts along the old fortified area, sipped Kir Royale at an outdoor café across from the magnificent Fairmont Le Château Frontenac (built by the Canadian railroad company in 1899) and dined on Quebec meat pies at Restaurant Aux Anciens Canadiens. By the time we got off the ramparts and seated for dinner, we felt like those anciens Canadians.

Lumbering into the campground here in Quebec, we were assigned a site directly overlooking the St. Lawrence. Out the back window of the RV we have the lazily moving waterway, hawks flying and black squirrels leaping. To the side Fay and Bonnie tried to light a campfire. I should have listened more in Girl Scouts instead of scouting the other scouts. We finally got it done, but it required burning all the magazines we had on board. Thankfully, sparks flew before my mate started eyeing copies of *For Frying Out Loud*.

This trip, our longest ever, has been, by necessity, different. We're cooking more in the RV since traveling for a month is no two week vacation and we're trying to stay out of debtor's prison. Luckily we have a grill and don't have to count on our suspect campfire girl skills.

Today, on a tip from the book *1000 Places to See Before You Die*, we drove to La Malbaie, in the mountains. The narrow, impossibly steep road up was so long and winding, I hoped it would not be a place we'd see right before we died.

At the summit we found yet another fairytale Fairmont Chateau with turrets and battlements and all manner of gables and things. Even though the weather turned nasty, with heavy rain, the vistas of the mountains running down to the river, socked-in with low-hanging clouds, provided quite a show. In just a few weeks they will start to get snow—22 feet each winter.

Then, on our way back to the campsite, we stopped at Chute Montmorency, a waterfall that is dramatically taller than Niagara Falls and ringed by a series of walkways. If the thundering falls doesn't take your breath away then the walk from the parking lot up to it will. We logged about a mile on the path and stairs up, crossed the falls on the somewhat scary footbridge and then headed down to the bottom via a series of switchback stairways. They reminded me of some kind of torture rack from the film *Bridge on the River Kwai*. I'd like to point out that once again we seemed to be the oldest people enjoying this particular adventure.

Me, at the bottom, panting like a St. Bernard: "I'd pay $12 not to have to walk back up."

Bonnie: "Why $12?"

Me: "That's what the tram back up costs."

We took the tram. Early night tonight. I think I have a full-body sprain.

August third or fourth, maybe

Driving eight hours today from Quebec to New Brunswick,

along the St. Lawrence, then inland. Amazing mountain and lake views. Passed the town of Saint-Louis-du-Ha! Ha!, the only municipality in North America with exclamation points in its name. Nobody seems to know from whence came the name.

From Ha! Ha! we passed a sign for the New Brunswick Potato Museum and I made Bonnie stop. Now she's seriously questioning taking me cross country.

We did pass up stops in towns featuring the world's largest axe and the site of the last official duel in North America. So many largests and lasts, so little time.

August 7

Made it to Fundy Park where we climbed down another ridiculous series of staircases to get to the floor of the bay, at low tide, where the gigantic 40-70 foot Hopewell Rocks stood exposed. These giant sculptures were formed by ages and ages of the largest tidal changes in the world. And it's amazing how fast you can climb back up those stairs when that huge tide starts coming back in.

August 8 (for a full report, turn the page)...▼

August 2013

August 9

Yesterday, we arrived in beautiful Chester, Nova Scotia, where we are visiting a friend in a house with spectacular water views. This morning said friend had me out walking three point five miles. Who is this typing and what have they done with Fay? We are having a positively grand time, even if I may need to detox from the great outdoors when we return.

August 14

Except for the 3-4 mile forced marches, we have had an amazingly relaxing time. We traveled across to the Northern shore one day for lunch at Lucketts Winery, where they have scrumptious food and drink, plus, in the middle of the vineyard, an old-fashioned English red phone booth. And, from it, you can call anywhere in the world for free. Hence, their most popular wine is Phone Box Red and Phone Box White.

For the past few days Bon and I did little but lounge on the deck reading (Bon), writing (me), and having a vacation from our vacation. By today a soupy fog rolled in. We could hardly see the drinks in our hands. We managed.

August 16

Now we get it when locals say there are two seasons here, winter and construction. We drove, through miles of road cones and flaggers to a teeny lake community in the center of Nova Scotia. We'd been invited to stay with two women we met last year at the campground in Lunenburg. They have a spectacular log home, decorated entirely in Southwestern Cowboy décor, with Georgia O'Keefe cattle skulls and boots and spurs everywhere. It's really a showplace, overlooking a small river and lake.

One of the cowgirls took me on my first all-terrain-vehicle ride and it was a doozy—we flew along snowmobile trails, through rutted roads and humongous mud puddles. I came back laughing, covered in terrain.

Canada is so cool. While the gals are the only lesbians in the community, back in June they threw a Pride Party and all their straight neighbors came in rainbow shirts. But the girls were sure glad to see us and have an opportunity to make U-Haul jokes, and chat about the fall of DOMA, Edie Windsor, and other topics their neighbors aren't apt to discuss.

Tomorrow we have plans for a ferry ride to Big Tancook Island, where they make sauerkraut.

August 17

Trip Advison.com will hear from us. We called the trip The Hunger Games. Took the 1 p.m. ferry to the island to discover only one restaurant, which appeared less than clean, with rude staff. Asked about the art gallery and we heard it was closed. That was IT…nothing else on the island! What about the sauerkraut? It seems that 25 years ago a couple of deer swam over from the mainland, went back, and told all their friends, and the herd came back to decimate the cabbage patch. No more sauerkraut. You'd think the islanders could manage to grow a head of cabbage or two during rutting season, but no.

So we walked around the island—FOR FOUR HOURS!—on dirt roads, amid a thundering barrage of pre-teens on ATVs, kicking up dust storms in our faces. A police car drove by, but when it got close we saw that the star on the door said BEER PATROL and the officers appeared to be bubbas. Cue the banjo music!

Got back to the ferry an hour early, 'cause believe me we did not want to miss it. And you could hear our stomachs rumbling over the ferry engines. Okay, some of the scenery was pretty, but jeesh, a trip to nowhere. I don't even want to think about Little Tancook Island. As for the editor of *1000 Places to See Before You Die*, her credibility is kaput.

August 18

Luxuriated at the waterfront and readied ourselves for the trip home. Cleaning out the RV fridge was like Survivor Nova Scotia, due to their complex and stringently regulated recycling system. There's a compost "wet" bin, a plastics/aluminum "dry" bin, a paper bin and, as if that's not enough to put me in the loony bin, a garbage pail for the rest. Panicked we'd goof, leaving a hostess gift of a $200 fine or jail, we drove to the grocery store and furtively—as furtive as you can be in a 27 foot recreational vehicle—started lobbing trash into what we hoped were the right slots. Luckily, Bonnie and Clyde weren't nabbed.

We've loved our stay in Nova Scotia and the two weeks before that in Montreal and Quebec...but we are happy to be heading home. The very last days of the trip, we had plenty of moxie. Read on and you will see why. ▼

No Walk in the Park

It started with the soap. A friend said her Mom often had nighttime leg spasms and somebody suggested she sleep with a bar of Dove soap in the bed to quell the cramps. Mom laughed until she tried it and reluctantly admitted it seemed to work.

So, after walking the hills and climbing the Quebec City ramparts, when my mate complained of an overnight charley horse, I returned from the store with a solution.

"I bought you a Dove Bar."

Her eyes lit up with a vision of the wrong kind of Dove Bar. Realizing my error, I quickly added "No, no, not ice cream, a bar of Dove soap!"

"Excuse me?" she stuttered, crestfallen.

"I heard that sleeping with a bar of Dove soap in bed can lessen or even prevent leg cramps."

Then it was her turn to laugh so hard she got a cramp in her side.

This episode would have been forgotten if it weren't for the cruelty of mapmakers in Fundy Park, Nova Scotia. The park map showed color-coded walks and hikes. A purple dotted line offered a short stroll "suitable for everyone." Surely we could up our game to the green level, promising a 2.5 kilometer walk, "comfortable for almost everyone."

Now look, I know I'm a senior citizen. I've been happily accepting discounts the whole trip. But the map specifically did not say "except you, grandma," and in fact went on to list three higher levels of black, brown and red walks in the park.

You know where this is going, which, obviously we didn't.

We started along the path, all alone in the forest, stepping between chunky roots and hefty rocks. About five minutes in my mate asked if I had bars on the cell phone. Was she concerned we'd finally see the moose we'd been hunting at the highway moose crossing signs?

From a path littered with tree roots and boulders, going straight downhill, I might add, the terrain changed with the addition of mud holes rivaling the La Brea tar pits. Crossing brooks and rivulets with ungainly Olympic broad jumps, I wondered just how gracefully the rest of the almost everybodys had handled this part of the green line.

Hearing foot traffic behind us, we were quickly overtaken by a pack of laughing twenty-somethings skipping down the rocky, rooted trail like it was the yellow brick road.

"I think the easy purple line meant for people over 30," I muttered.

"You want to turn back before we see the waterfalls?"

"No, in for a penny, in for a hip replacement."

We continued our downward spiral through gunky mud puddles and giant root canals when I stopped to take a few notes on my iPhone.

"What are you doing?"

"Channeling Henry David Thoreau. Walden Pond was probably a dotted purple line."

When we came to a clearing with a great big toppled tree across the path I tripped getting over it. If Fay falls in the forest and there's no one there to laugh is it still humiliating? Yes, yes it is.

Now mind you, this whole time we hadn't seen anybody coming back *up* the trail. We had gotten an early start, but the lack of return trippers did worry me. Finally, a family with fit-looking parents and two fit-looking teenage boys rose from the depths, looking no worse for wear. Their golden doodle wasn't so lucky. The poor thing was panting and drooling with his tongue hanging out.

When they were safely out of earshot my loving mate said "I hate to tell you, but right now you're looking a little like that doodle dog."

I would have said something snarky but I was too busy panting and drooling.

194

Finally, we made it to the falls, where those twenty-some-things were swimming and laughing. We took the requisite photos of the falls and steeled ourselves to head back up the green mile and three quarters. It was agony to realize that 2.5K had been only half the ordeal.

Without going into further torturous detail, the climb out of the great dismal swamp took a long time and was very nearly our waterloo. Not only were we exhausted but, having been drinking water like good hikers, a loo was exactly what we needed. I knew if we followed time honored tradition to stop in the woods to relieve ourselves, that's exactly when other hikers would catch us with our proverbial and actual pants down.

So we soldiered on, taking as much time as our bladders would allow, hoisting ourselves back up to civilization. Reaching the parking lot, we patted ourselves on the back for a job well done. Also to stop the coughing.

I cannot imagine hiking the park's black or brown dotted routes and the thin red line must be for mountain goats and mental cases. And speaking of craziness, I'm back at the bar of soap thing again.

Later, as our sinews stiffened from exertion followed by hours of sitting on our butts around the glorious campfire, it was time for lights out.

"Hey," I said, feeling the first twinges of leg cramps. "Hand over the Dove bar."

And for the first time ever, I would not have preferred chocolate.▼

September 2013

For a carbonated soft drink I didn't taste until recently, *Moxie—Distinctively Different*, has played an enormous role in my life.

By my late twenties, I'd heard the vocabulary word "moxie" of course, a noun synonymous for determination, courage and spunk. And at the time, I'd surely lost mine. I was fleeing a suffocating marriage, questioning my sexuality and had pretty much nowhere to go.

I was a scared, closeted lesbian in her twenties, who showed up on the doorstep of a liberal, socially conscious, recently widowed, heterosexual friend in her mid-fifties. I stood there with two cat-carriers (inhabited), the clothes on my back and the need for a place to reinvent myself.

My friend Mary Jane invited me to make a nest in the basement of her home and I stayed for over four years. We'd been casual friends before but became grand lifelong family members.

I adored Mary Jane's wicked sense of humor and her adventurous nature. She taught me to drink booze without mixers, got me to grow up a little, proved absolutely non-judgmental in a hostile and homophobic world, and gave me the courage and good-natured push to come out of the closet.

Gay male friends took us both drinking and disco-ing at DC's Lost and Found and other glitzy 70s gay bars, where we had Saturday night fever and loved the night life, loved to boogie.

Back at home. Mary Jane had an elderly Schnauzer named Max, who I also came to adore. After he passed, she brought home one determined, spunky Schnauzer puppy which she promptly named Moxie.

One day, Mary Jane and I wandered into an antique store to find an old embossed bottle that said Moxie Nerve Food on it. A hobby was born, as we discovered the history of the New

England soft drink called Moxie and started trolling antique stores seeking Moxie memorabilia. We collected cans, bottles, ad posters, paper fans and promotional materials. We even found a wooden Moxie yardstick.

Enter Bonnie. By 1982, Mary Jane had had a ringside seat to much of my coming out angst and dyke dating dramas. Mary Jane liked my lesbian and gay pals and she especially liked Bonnie when she came into my life. We all partied together and Mary Jane loved her status as mother hen and token straight.

When Bonnie and I bought our first home, I left most of my Moxie memorabilia behind with Mary Jane and she sent us off with a puppy sired by Moxie as a housewarming gift. The housewarming gift was more of a house wetting gift and we named the little pisher Max so the cycle could begin again.

For the next twenty years or more, we dined weekly with Mary Jane, often sought her advice and counsel and especially sought out antique stores on our New England travels to enhance her Moxie collection.

In 1998, just before we lost our beloved Max to old age, we'd gotten a Schnauzer puppy, and of course, his name had to be Moxie. A year later, our second puppy arrived with the name Paddy and we just went with it.

Clearly, along with my Moxie memorabilia compulsion, Mary Jane also gets alternating credit and blame for my Schnauzer addiction.

Bonnie and I remained close to Mary Jane through the years, until she passed away in 2005, taking with her a large chunk of my heart. Aside from the legacy of dog names and breed specificity she left me boxes of Moxie memorabilia. Our home has had a certain Moxie decorating panache for years.

My Moxie and Paddy are gone now too, and Bonnie and I are on temporary Schnauzer hiatus.

Ironically, just a few weeks ago, preparing for our downsizing move, I hosted a yard sale and sold most of the Moxie items to a collector who was thrilled to have them. I kept the original embossed Moxie Nerve Food bottle, the Moxie yard stick and the memories.

But here's the astonishing thing. On the last day of our Canada/Maine vacation, a Wednesday, we saw a sign for the Union Blueberry Fest, happening about 15 minutes from our Maine campground.

On a complete whim, we drove to the fair, where, at the entrance, we saw a banner across the road. *Wednesday is Moxie Day!* it said, in the logo print of the soft drink. I grinned.

"What does that mean?" I asked the ticket-seller.

"Oh, at the museum, free samples of Moxie today."

Museum? Yes, it was the Blueberry Fest, like a state fair, with goats and chickens, a midway and funnel cakes. But on the fairgrounds stood the Matthews Museum of Maine Heritage, featuring "our extensive Moxie Collection."

I'd say it's the largest Moxie Museum in the world, but I have a feeling it's the only Moxie Museum in the world. The entire exhibit hall, almost as big as the RB Convention Center, was crammed with thousands upon thousands of Moxie bottles, ads, posters, soda wagons, soda fountain signs, crates, antique photographs and objects I'd never seen before.

Having inadvertently stepped into paradise, I chatted with the docents and learned about all things Moxie. Among the plethora of treasures and memorabilia, I was stunned to learn they do not have a single Moxie yardstick.

Needless to say, I spent much more time at the museum than at the blueberry spitting contest or the oxen vs. tractor pull (although that was a first for me). And I bought a bright orange souvenir Moxie hat and orange Moxie museum shirt. The staff, thrilled to have a visitor so fascinated with the collection, gave me several complimentary orange Moxie stickers, a drink cooler and more. As the new TV series says, orange IS the new black, so I'm all set.

Oh, and I tasted Moxie soda. Let's just say it's a cross between Coke and root beer, with quite a bit of fizz. I have a feeling it's been sweetened over the years to satisfy the contemporary palate. In the old days, to earn the moniker nerve food, it probably had a lot more, well, moxie.

So I'm still reeling from the lucky coincidence that had us in the backwoods of Maine, stumbling across a Moxie Museum on Moxie Day, so I could indulge in this mini Moxie memoir.

We're heading home this morning. And when I get home, the first thing I will do is donate that Moxie yard stick to the museum. Downsizing, you know. In fact, from the minute we arrive home, we have ten, count 'em, ten days to pack and vacate the house. On your mark...▼

September 2013

We're home, working frantically to get the hell out of one house and into another. And I am having a figurative attack of Mercury poisoning.

All I know about mercury I learned from my 7th grade science teacher. I know it's a tiny planet, often called Quicksilver, and an element on that periodic chart. It's found in fish and the silver stuff in thermometers, which wiggles around the floor if you break the glass. Oh, and there was Freddie Mercury, but he's gone now. Ditto the Mercury auto, now extinct. Yes, I've heard the phrase, "Mercury is in retrograde," from astrology, but that's a subject about which I am clueless.

Back in the 60s when everybody asked "What's your sign," I'd piss off the hippies by answering "slippery when wet."

But after the week I've had, when somebody suggested my problems might be caused by Mercury being in retrograde, I was willing to give it a cursory nod.

Apparently, when Mercury is in retrograde, which has something to do with an illusion that it's moving backward through the sky, our plans go awry. Bad stuff happens. Specifically, one astrologer reported, that since Mercury governs all transportation and communication issues (who knew?), anything to do with those areas can go maddeningly wrong. And this year, the planet was in retrograde at the exact time when every communication, transportation or even plumbing device I owned broke.

First came the iPhone. The Verizon store couldn't fix it, making me iRate. Fuming, I came out to the parking lot and my electronic key wouldn't open the car door. I had to dig the lock open like a safecracker with the tiny metal stick buried in the fob. That set off the car alarm which launched me into a frantic hunt for the button to shut it off.

A snide teen in the lot had fun yelling "Help! This car is

being stolen!!!" and by the time I shut down the screaming buzzer and retreated to the steaming hot car I was humiliated as well as irate. When I ordered a new electronic key for the car it cost almost as much as the iPhone. I want a key, not the whole freaking door panel.

Next, as I drove toward Annapolis and an address I'd never visited, Mercury did what the Incredible Hulk couldn't. It detached the Velcro from my windshield, allowing the EZ-pass device to commit suicide by landing on the floor of the car, where I stepped on it as I accelerated.

By the time I realized Mercury had my GPS in retrograde too, I was headed for an address from a month ago, requiring me to cross the Bay Bridge a second time to right myself. I had plenty of time in the cash line on the bridge to dig the EZ-Pass pieces out of the driver's side foot well.

Back home, as we prepared to empty the house for our move, I pushed print on one last document and my computer printer, after a decade of exemplary service, ate a ream of paper. I watched in horror as it disgorged pages around the room, gagging and choking and grinding to a halt. There's nothing half so stupid as using two hands to try and yank a wad of paper from an inanimate object and losing the fight.

On the day before we moved, I made the error of flushing a Kleenex down the guest bathroom toilet, and after 14 years of exemplary service, water gushed from the base of the device.

"Dammit, we need a wax ring!" hollered my mate. Now there's an item I'd never shopped for before. Minutes later I'm in the Lowes plumbing department grabbing for the wax ring (so unlike the carousel's brass ring) so we could spend the next hour power lifting the porcelain horse and trying to reset it. That's the Royal we. I just watched in fascination.

Following that episode, the vacuum stopped sucking, which totally sucked. Not only did it not inhale, but it spewed last month's dirt all over the living room like a scene from some Ken Burns' dust bowl documentary. If Mercury in retrograde is the illusion of moving backward, we were suddenly worried we wouldn't be moving at all.

I was cleaning up the vacuum dirt with a broom, when my Sirius radio remote quit working. It stranded the radio broadcasting the XM Sex Channel, which previous to the panting sounds I heard, I never knew existed. I was so startled by someone panting louder than I was at the vacuuming, I ripped my earbuds out and broke them.

Okay, Mercury baby, this has to stop. Thinking there was some credence to this whole planet moving backwards stuff I consulted that paragon of factual integrity, the internet. After wading through pages of astrological advice to the lovelorn and Zodiac based investment tips, I froze at this sentence: "We don't tend to get all the information we need at this time, so it can be hard to make big decisions; it's not always the best time to sign a contract, either."

Great. What about the real estate settlement? OMG.

Luckily, Mercury stayed at the old house and all went according to plan. But I was still wary of the following internet warning: "Mercury also rules industries like publishing, writing and editing."

Great. Now Mercury is my editor? When I push send on this column, will my real editor actually receive it? It's enough to give me a low retrograde fever. My apologies to the astrologists among us. Like for Tinkerbell, I am clapping my hands. I believe. ▼

October 2013

My only blood-relative first cousin passed away this week. He was only 66 which was hideously depressing. But he had been in poor cardiac health for years, so it wasn't quite the shock it might have been.

I loved Kenn dearly; he was really, really odd in a fabulous way. A bona fide opera and theatre junkie, Kenn, a rotund funny man, quick with a naughty joke and even quicker with opera and Broadway trivia, knew how to make us laugh. And think. As Rabbi Sharon Kleinbaum from New York's gay synagogue said at his service, he was a humanist, a classical, Renaissance scholar devoted to our world and the people in it.

However, scholar and writer, though he be, the rabbi knew he was not above loudly and flamboyantly booing Maria Callas at the Met or standing up at the family Thanksgiving table singing, "I Yam, what I Yam" in a Harvey Fierstein baritone. Graveside, the rabbi mentioned that she hoped when he got to where his soul was going, he would meet up with his idol, singer Renata Tebaldi, and the two of them would be able to avoid Maria Callass.

We have so many Kenn memories. Opera queen direct from the womb, after one holiday meal he had himself, me, and my sister, ages 11, 10 and 7 respectively, perform the last act of *Tosca*, including miming its famed acts of torture, murder and suicide. We had no idea what we were doing, but Puccini would have been so proud. Or perhaps nauseas. I have no recollection of the looks on my parents' faces, but perhaps that's good.

When Kenn's funky New York neighborhood started to gentrify, with dozens of upscale boutiques arriving, he announced he was surprised the funeral home didn't change its name to Death and Things.

And whenever anybody had a birthday, you'd get a call

announcing, "This is Ethel Merman calling from the great beyond to wish you a Happy Birthday." Kenn would then launch into the Happy Birthday song in his very exaggerated Ethel Merman voice. It was a tradition. It might have been what caused the break-up of Bell telephone.

I tell you all this because, one, I'm sad and I wanted you to know a little about my quirky cousin. Things like he once was crossing the street and hit a car. Broadsided it. Crumpled the whole side panel. He was fine. In fact, his mother took him, in her words "to get his head examined and they found nothing." Laughed over that for years.

In the 70s there was a gay magazine in New York called *Michael's Thing* (honest), where he wrote a popular opera column. At first he proudly called himself the only straight writer at *Michael's Thing*. One day he just called himself a writer at *Michael's Thing*. His having dropped the bomb to the family first gave me the courage to come out.

But I'm writing now to tell you about the very last Kenn experience I had. It was a gift.

I drove up to New York the night before his funeral by myself since, for a combination of good reasons, Bonnie could not join me. I borrowed a friend's apartment for the night and faced the prospect of a evening alone in Manhattan. What could be bad?

I took a taxi from my digs in Chelsea, just above the Village, up to Times Square, soaking up the frenetic billboards, throngs of people and general mad hysteria of the scene.

As a tribute to Kenn, I took myself to dinner at Juniors, a deli harkening back to its start in 1950s Brooklyn and Miami Beach. As my cousin would have done, I ordered a towering chopped liver sandwich on rye. It recalled the rhetorical question "What am I, chopped liver?" to which the answer, in Kenn's case, might have been yes, the cholesterol adding to his coronary woes. In his honor I only ate half.

From there, on this clear, comfortable, October night I walked to Sixth Avenue, heading for Bryant Park behind the

New York library. From ten blocks away I could see pink lights projected up into the trees and, the closer I got, the more music and cheering I heard. It was an outdoor Shakira concert, which I joined, standing to watch the performer, the videos and the light show. At one point I looked to the right and saw the lit spire of the art deco Chrysler Building and to the left, the pink-lit upper floors of the Empire State Building. Breast Cancer Awareness Month. New York was in the pink.

Traveling south, back towards Chelsea, I passed Herald Square, as in George M. Cohan's "Give My Regards to Broadway, Remember Me to Herald Square." There stood Macy's, the biggest department store in the world, with—here comes the strange—a long lap pool erected in front of the store, where Macy's was hosting Nyad Swims for Superstorm Sandy Relief.

That baby boomer lesbian dynamo, Diana Nyad, who had just completed the history-making swim from Cuba to Key West, had vowed to swim 40 hours without stopping to raise money for the victims of the devastating storm.

I stepped forward off the street, up two steps of temporary bleachers and leaned over the side of the pool. Diana Nyad, in a pink bathing cap, swam by me so closely I could have reached out and patted her on the back. I wanted to. An inspiration.

Moving on, I was approached by several aggressive panhandlers, homeless I suspect, but I did not stop to fill their coffers. My favorite sign, however, was "Why Lie? Need Beer." Several blocks later I did spy a woman who appeared to be homeless, camped on the street with her small dog. I handed her a twenty. It just felt right.

By the time I walked the 28 blocks back to my lodging, my spirit was willing to continue but not the soles of my feet. I briefly considered going to the Stonewall Inn or Marie's Crisis piano bar in the Village, but I came to my senses.

Upstairs I went, and walked out onto the apartment's balcony, overlooking the still-busy, brightly lit and noisy streets below. It was fun being part of it, New York, New York. I popped the metal tab on a diet Coke and toasted to Cousin Kenn. Thanks, buddy for an amazing night on the town in NYC.

I can't believe I won't ever get a Mermangram again.▼

October 2013

Down, Not Out in Resort Heaven

So, we are downsized. Some friends and acquaintances think we are insane for giving up our home on three quarters of an acre in exchange for a partially double-wide, partially single-wide mobile home (trailer) in a community where we don't own the land.

Hey, they do the lawn here. We're happy as clams. I saw the first leaf drop the other day and laughed like a hyena. I drove by my old house and saw the tree service juggling tools at the roof line. I guffawed. The notice that it's time to open up the irrigation system was forwarded to my new address. I crumpled it up and made a three-pointer to the circular file.

I also dropped my gym membership since this community has an exercise room with treadmills, bikes and an elliptical machine. It's just as easy and a lot cheaper for me not to go here as not to go there.

I admit that there were many things that had to be done in the new house to make it comfortable and attractive. Uninhabited for a year when we purchased it, the place was a true fixer-upper. Since I am not a fixer-upper, the work was mostly tasked to my spouse.

In her quest to guild the turd, Bonnie installed ceiling moldings, all new light fixtures, faucets, switch plates and the like. What a wonderful difference! And she painted every single wall in the house, hiding the 1980s floral and speckled vinyl wall covering favored in that era.

Frankly, getting this place put together was such a job she had to enlist me for physical labor as well.

Clearly, you understand how massive the job had to be for her to resort to the nuclear option.

So she gave me a paintbrush, with instructions to finish painting some unpainted furniture for my office. "Put on paint clothes first," she cautioned. Like I would have any.

Paint roller in hand I went to work with all the gusto of passengers diving off the Titanic. I obsessed over the top of a shelf unit until I realized nobody would see it unless dinner guests included members of the NBA.

First Law of Semi-Gloss: Only after your hands become covered with dripping paint will your nostril itch. Corollary: and then you have to pee.

Okay, so I'm not a great painter. If I'd been using red paint it would have looked like the St. Valentines Day Massacre. Bring on the splatter expert. Bonnie took one look and relieved me of my duties.

Next, she asked me if I wanted to screw, which sounded great until I discovered it meant installing new kitchen cabinet hardware. *Newton's Law: any screw you drop will immediately roll under the heaviest appliance.* I spent quite some time on my hands and knees fetching like a golden retriever.

In one instance I was leaning over the stove, reaching for an errant screw, when my shirt tail caught on a knob, turning on a burner. Luckily it's an electric stove. If it was my old propane stove I would have immolated myself. *Dumbo's Law of Averages: The chance of being watched while you work is directly proportional to how dumb the thing is you are doing.*

At that point Bonnie told me to get down and find her some real lesbians to help.

We'd been in the house 23 days and to Lowes 27 times. Mostly me, searching for the one thing Bonnie forgot to get for the project already in progress. We're there so often the hot dog man knows us by name and we are welcome to use the employee lounge .

And we've made friends with Ellen from the paint department. Relationships develop quickly when a clerk has to be the arbiter between people arguing over Latte Semi-Gloss vs. Desert Beige Satin.

When our new appliances were delivered, we found that one half inch of counter top obstructed installation of the new fridge. Bonnie promptly revved up her reciprocal saw and, to the amazement of the delivery guys, sliced off the offending formica.

We met our waterloo at the Microwave. Installed with the original cabinetry, it would have hung down so far we could only have cooked flat food in frying pans. Steady diet of flatbread and fritattas, anyone?

For this project we hired pros to tune-up our kitchen. The two gentlemen were great, improvising a cabinet on its side to hang the microwave and figuring out an ingenious method of venting it out. Yes, they were here for days, and we were beginning to think of them like Eldin the painter-in-residence on the old *Murphy Brown* series, but they did a great job.

For a while of course, Bonnie, who was out and proud from the moment of birth I believe, was a closet case. She spent at least a week in the master bedroom closet installing various closet stretchers, closet helpers and closet do-dads trying to buy us more space.

And by today, deadline day for *Letters*, we have been in the house exactly 32 days. We are pleased with the progress and pooped at the same time. Somebody on the internet coined a word that describes our condition perfectly. Exhaustipated. Too tired to give a shit.

But we love our new home. Out the corner of my eye I just spied the landscape brigade heading our way. Oy, I feel smug. Don't exhaustipate yourselves, fellas.▼

Epilogue

I follow Suze Orman's advice. If you are going to spend your money, spend it on people first, experiences second and things third. Words to live by. And we are.

With the sale of our humongous sea of grass with the little house on the prairie on it, and our move to the "manufactured home," which I am getting used to saying instead of "trailer," life is good.

Like Susie says, we're spending on us, and in some cases our friends, first. Experiences, like an upcoming trip to the Galapagos Islands second. And stuff third, although we are trying to wean ourselves off Lowes and Bed, Bath & Beyond.

When the travel folks at *1000 Places to See.com* recently came out with a list of the top 100, Bonnie and I had already managed to scratch off 33 sites on the list. Our January cruise to see penguins and Blue-Footed Boobies will get us to 34. If all goes well, and we accomplish our planned 2015 cross country RV adventure, lots of numbers will fall.

Back when my first book was published, and I started to get notes and e-mails from readers from all over the map, I said I hoped that someday we could go cross-country, visiting. That day is approaching. I would love to see how our tribe is doing in various places around the country. I am well aware that life in Rehoboth, or Gayberry RFD as we call it, is unique. Sometimes, when I hear sad tales from other parts of the country I know we are in a diversity bubble, unlike much of the nation. Goodness knows, I never expected Delaware to be in the vanguard like it is. Strange and wonderful things have happened here.

And while this book is putting to pasture the Frying Series (unless I can't stifle my urge to write a prequel called *A Kiss Before Frying*), I suspect I have not used up my words yet. As we set out in the RV, or on a plane, train or in the car, I think there will be stories. After all, we're seriously considering a puppy come spring.

In the meantime, thanks for reading. It means the world to me. I look forward to seeing you on facebook, at book signings, in P-Town, in Rehoboth Beach or anywhere our travels take us.

Most of all, here's to our ability to laugh rather than moan.

Just last night I opened a fortune cookie that said "you will soon be surrounded by good friends and laughter."

Who could ask for anything more?▼

Fall 2013

ACKNOWLEDGEMENTS

I thought I was done as a trilogy, but no, many people urged me to keep going. Thanks!

Naturally, thanks, again, to my wife Bonnie (who, this year, is finally, my wife in the eyes of the IRS and other federal agencies) for willing, so often, to be represented in print, despite the remarks or questions publication may produce at Happy Hour.

Thanks once again to Steve Elkins and Murray Archibald, of CAMP Rehoboth, who keep me in ink. They work harder and become more selfless each year as they give back to the community in Rehoboth Beach. They are both so incredibly talented it's ridiculous. And I love them more every day. Thanks, too, to Terry Plowman and all my new readers at *Delaware Beach Life*, and Maribeth Fishcher and my friends at the Rehoboth Beach Writer's Guild — they encourage me.

Gratitude goes to my perceptive and speedy draft readers, Kathy Galloway and Fran Sneider—I can always count on you when it comes to comments large ("You don't really want to say this in print, do you?") or small ("you never met a comma you didn't love.")

To Eric, the man who permits me to be a Jewish mother, all my thanks and love, always. Diversity are us, kiddo.

And, once again, a very special nod to my dear friend and new neighbor Stefani Deoul for telling me, mostly via international calls, when my tales go awry and being perceptive enough, not to mention willing, to suggest how to fix them.

I really do get by with a little help from my friends.

Lastly, to my *Letters from CAMP Rehoboth* readers, I love you for still being there even after all these years. We're closing in on two decades. And 2013 has been a doozey—for me personally and for all of us as a community.

An enormous hug to you all.

A NOTE ABOUT THE AUTHOR

Fay Jacobs, a native New Yorker, spent 30 years in the Washington, DC area working in journalism, theater, and public relations. Her first book, *As I Lay Frying—a Rehoboth Beach Memoir* was published in 2004 and is in its third printing. Her second, *Fried & True—Tales from Rehoboth Beach* was released in 2007. That book won the 2008 Golden Crown Literary Society Award for non-fiction and was recognized by the National Federation of Press Women as 2008 Book of the Year for Humor. *For Frying Out Loud—Rehoboth Beach Diaries*, released in 2010 won a slew of awards, including the American Library Association Over the Rainbow nomination and National Federation of Press Women Humor Book of the Year. Fay has contributed feature stories and columns to such publications as *The Washington Post*, *The Advocate*, *OutTraveler*, *curve* magazine, *The Baltimore Sun*, *Chesapeake Bay Magazine*, *The Washington Blade*, *The Wilmington News Journal*, *Delaware Beach Life* and more.

Since 1995 she has been a regular columnist for *Letters from CAMP Rehoboth*, and won the national 1997 Vice Versa Award for excellence.

She and Bonnie, her partner of 30 years and wife of one year, live in Rehoboth Beach, Delaware.

A NOTE ABOUT THE PUBLISHER

A&M Books was established in 1995 by the late Anyda Marchant and Muriel Crawford. Prior to starting A&M Books, Marchant and Crawford were two of the founders of the legendary feminist publishing house Naiad Press.

A&M Books is the publisher of the fourteen classic Sarah Aldridge novels, along with books by Fay Jacobs, the 2005 release of *Celebrating Hotchclaw* by feminist literary icon Ann Allen Shockley, and its newest authors, Stefani Deoul, who wrote the novel *The Carousel* and J. Lee Watton with her Don't Ask, Don't Tell memoir *Out of Step*.